CW00839258

Dedicated to
OSHO
by the gracious
gift of
Ann Palm.

**CHIDVILAS, INC**

*Bhagwan Shree Rajneesh*
*is now simply known*
*as Osho.*

The word **Osho** is derived from William James' expression
'oceanic experience' which means dissolving into the ocean.
**'Osho'** is also a term derived from ancient Japanese,
often used by disciples to address their masters.

**'O'** means *"with great respect, love and gratitude"*
as well as *"synchronicity"* and *"harmony."*
**'Sho'** means *"multidimensional expansion of consciousness"*
and *"existence showering from all directions."*

**Osho** is an enlightened master of our time.
All the words printed here are spoken
words spontaneously addressed to an audience of
thousands of seekers from around the world.

# Osho

# After Middle Age:
## A Limitless Sky

Published by Chidvilas, Inc
PO Box 17550, Boulder, CO
80308 USA

Copyright © Osho International Foundation
Rennweg 34, 8001 Zurich, Switzerland

Cover Design by: Ma Amrit Mary, B.F.A.

Compiled by: Mary Amoore, Q.S.M.

First Edition 1989 Hazard Press
Second Edition 1992 Chidvilas, Inc.

Printed by Johnson Printing, Boulder, Colorado.

ISBN 0-918963-02-8

# TABLE OF CONTENTS

## Part One

## Part Two

## Part Three

# PART ONE

# Time for Change

IN EACH PERSON'S life the times of change come, and one of the greatest things to remember is that when you change a certain pattern of life, you have to change naturally. It is not in your hands.

Biology makes you capable of sex at the age of thirteen or fourteen – it is not your doing. At a certain age, as you are coming closer to forty, or forty-two, biology's purpose is finished. All those hormones that have been propelling you are disappearing. To accept this change is very difficult; you suddenly start thinking as if you are no longer beautiful, that you need a face lift.

I have heard about a woman who was telling a plastic surgeon that she needed a face lift. The surgeon looked at her and said, "There is nothing wrong, it is just age, don't be worried about it. Why unnecessarily go to the trouble?" But the woman was insistent, so the doctor said, "Okay. But it will cost you five thousand dollars." The woman said, "That much money I don't have. Can't you suggest something cheaper?" The doctor said, "Yes. You can purchase a veil."

It is one of the Western problems. In the East no woman is worried, things are accepted as they come. Acceptance has been the basic foundation of Eastern life: the West is continuously imposing on nature, demanding how things should be. Nobody wants to become old. So when the time of transition from one stage of life comes, a very strange phenomenon happens: just as a candle comes to the very end and there are only a few seconds more and it will be gone, at the last moment the candle suddenly becomes bigger, with all its power. Nobody wants to go.

It is a fact well-known to medical science that at the time of death people suddenly become completely healthy. All their diseases disappear. This is the last effort of their life – to resist death.

The people who are related to them feel very happy that suddenly all diseases have disappeared, the person has become calm and quiet; but they don't know it signifies death. The diseases have disappeared because their function is fulfilled, they have killed the man. Now, it is the last spurt of life.

The same happens with every biological change in life. When sex is becoming irrelevant, you start thinking of sex more than ever, and suddenly, a great spurt! Because so much sexuality is suddenly overwhelming the mind, the mind can only understand logically, rationally one thing – from where is this sexuality coming? – it must be coming from the repressed unconscious.

That is what Sigmund Freud and his followers have been teaching to the whole world. They are right on many points. They are wrong on many points, particularly about the time of transition when you are no longer young and the hormones in you are going to disappear, and the interest in sex is going to die. Before dying it will explode with its full force, and if you go to a psychoanalyst he will say that you are sexually repressed.

I cannot say that, because I know that this sudden overwhelming sexuality will be gone by itself, you don't have to do anything; it is the signal that life is passing through a change. Now, life will be more calm and more quiet. You are really entering into a better state.

Sex is a little childish. As you become more and more mature, sex loses its grip over you. And it is a good sign. It is something to be happy about. It is not a problem to be solved, it is something to celebrate.

In the East no woman ever feels troubled by the transition from youth to old age. In fact she feels immensely happy that now that old demon is gone and life can be more peaceful. But the West has been living under many illusions. One is the illusion that there is only one life – that creates immense trouble. If there is only one life, and sex is disappearing, you are finished. Now there is no more opportunity, there will not be any more excitement in life. Nobody is going to say, "You are beautiful and I love you and I will love you forever."

So, first the illusion of one life creates a problem. Second, the psychoanalysts and other therapists have created another illusion – that sex is almost synonymous with life. The more sexual you are, the more alive you are. So when sex starts disappearing one starts feeling like a used cartridge. Now there is no point in living, life ends with sex ending. And then people try all kinds of bizarre things – face lifts, plastic surgery, false breasts... It is stupid, simply stupid. People start trying wigs. They start trying dresses which are sexually provoking.

Almost all Western women are starving – they call it dieting – because the idea in the West is that a woman is beautiful if she is not fat. Nature has some other idea. The woman has to be a little fat, because the woman, for nature, is a mother. A mother needs extra fat for the child, because when the child is in her womb he will need food, and when the child is in the womb the mother starts feeling nausea, she cannot eat, she starts throwing up. She needs emergency fat in her body so she can feed the child, because the child needs food; he is growing fast.

Science says that during the nine months in the mother's womb, a child grows faster than he will ever grow again in his seventy years of life. So fast...in nine months he passes through almost the whole evolution of man, from the fish – all the stages. His requirements have to be fulfilled by the mother, and she cannot eat. You can imagine, it is troublesome to have a child in your belly. I don't think any man would be ready to be pregnant. He would commit suicide without any doubt! He would jump from a fifty-story building – "Pregnant? I am finished."

Just think of the idea that you have a child in your belly, and you will go crazy. But how to get rid of it? The mother goes through immense suffering, great sacrifice.

Hence, in the East, we have not created the idea of a skinny woman. Of course the skinny woman looks more sexually attractive, younger. The fat woman looks less sexually interesting, because she loses proportion. Her waist is no more very small. Her body has gathered so much fat that nobody will feel attracted towards her. She does not have the necessary attraction for the human mind.

Just the other day somebody brought me a book of pictures taken by a famous photographer, and just on the front page is Sophia Loren. In the East she cannot be conceived of as very beautiful; she must be dieting, and dieting is nothing but the rich man's idea of starvation. Poor people starve by themselves;

rich people starve in a costly way, under professional guidance.

The fear is that you will not be attractive, that you will not be looked at by people any more. You will pass along the street and nobody will look back: "Who is going by?" To have attention is a great need for mankind, and particularly for women. Attention is nourishment. A woman suffers immensely when nobody pays attention to her. She has nothing else to attract people with, she has only her body. Man has not allowed her to develop other dimensions, whereby she can become a famous painter or a dancer or a singer or a learned professor. Man has cut all the other dimensions from a woman's life through which she could be attractive and people would pay respect to her even while she becomes old.

I have to remind you about the meaning of "respect." It means looking back. When somebody passes by, "re-spect." It has nothing to do with honor. It has something to do with the fact that you are suddenly aware that a beautiful thing has passed.

Woman is left by man with only a body – so she is much concerned with the body. That creates clinging, possessiveness, fear that if the person who loves her leaves, perhaps she will not find another. Without attention she starts feeling almost dead; what is the use of life if nobody pays attention to you? She does not have an intrinsic life of her own. Man has taught her that her life depends on others' opinions about her.

You see that all over the world beauty competitions are arranged only for women – and women do not even revolt against the idea. Why not for men? Just as you choose a Mrs. or Miss Universe, choose a Mr. Universe. No, nobody bothers about a man's body. He can grow fat, he can become Winston Churchill; he still attracts attention because he has power. In the same book, just next to Sophia Loren is standing Winston Churchill. Ugly, as fat as you can conceive, his whole face hanging – *he* needs a face lift, not Sophia Loren. But he will not bother. There is no need. He can have power, he can be the prime minister, he can be this and he can be that.

Man has managed over the centuries to have all the other dimensions of attracting people. And he has left only one dimension to woman – her body. He has made woman just a vegetable – and naturally the vegetable starts being worried if there are no customers! It is not a coincidence that in the most sexually perverted country, France, people say when they are in love with a woman, "I want to eat you." Are these people cannibals? Is the woman a vegetable, or what? "I want to eat you," shows a great respect for the woman! When nobody says to her, "I want to eat you," she thinks "I am now finished. Life has come to an end."

What you have to learn is first, a deep acceptance of all the changes that nature brings you. Youth has its own beauty, old age has its own beauty too. It may not be sexual, but if a man has lived silently, peacefully, meditatively, then old age will have a grandeur of its own. Just as the snow-covered peaks look beautiful, the white hairs of old age also have their own beauty. Not only beauty, but wisdom too, which no young man can claim, because all his behavior is stupid. He is running after this woman, running after that woman... The old man has stopped all this running business. He has settled in himself; he is no more dependent on anybody else. The old woman should follow the same way. There should be no difference between men and women.

Love happens only when you are beyond biological slavery. The biological relationship is so ugly that for centuries people have decided to make love in darkness, without light, so they don't see what they are doing.

When life is going through a biological change, it is not only to be accepted, it has to be rejoiced in that you have passed through all that stupidity, that now you are free from biological bondage. It is only a question of conditioning...

I have heard an ancient story – Arabic. A man's father died, and all the old men of the neighborhood came and said, "Don't be worried, son, if you have lost your father. We are here; don't think for a single moment that you are fatherless. We are all your fathers. You can always come to us with any difficulty, any problem."

He was very much consoled, seeing the concern of his neighbors. He had never thought that they would be so considerate. And then his mother died, and all the old women came and said, "Don't be worried, we are still alive. You can look upon us as your mother, and whatever your mother was doing for you, we can do. There is no problem about it."

He was very much consoled. And then his wife died. And not a single wife from the neighborhood came, to say, "Don't be worried, we are here. Whatever your wife was doing, we will do!"

The man was very angry. He stood in front of his house, watching to see if anybody comes or not, and nobody came. Finally he started shouting, "You nasty people! When my father died all the old men came; when my mother died all the old women came; and now my wife has died and no young woman is coming. What kind of neighborhood is this? Absurd, illogical! I have been waiting since the morning for somebody to turn up, but nobody has come."

One has to accept life. But your unconsciousness does not allow you to accept life as it is – you want something else.

It is perfectly good when sex disappears. You will be more capable of being alone. You will be more capable of being blissful, without any misery, because the whole game of sex is nothing but a long misery – fighting, hate, jealousy, envy. It is not a peaceful life.

And it is peace, silence, blissfulness, aloneness, freedom, which give you the real taste of what life is.

The Invitation, Session 24, September 2, 1987

# Osho,
*It has finally come to my consciousness that I am sexually repressed. Now I feel imprisoned by it and need your guidance.*

Don't be worried about repression: You are coming to the age when everybody feels disturbed, particularly women from the West. Middle age is a troublesome, anguish-creating state.

A few things for you to contemplate... First, one has to recognize that one is getting into middle-age:

Middle age is when you still believe you will feel better in the morning.

Middle age is when you want to see how long your car will last, instead of how fast it will go.

Middle age is when you are home on Saturday night, the telephone rings, and you hope it is not for you.

Middle age is when you change from stud to dud.

Middle age is when you stop criticizing the older generation and start criticizing the younger one.

These are just symptoms I am telling you...

The Invitation, Session 23, September 1, 1987

# Love and Alchemy

$\mathcal{M}$Y OWN UNDERSTANDING is that as your love deepens, your sex disappears. Love is so fulfilling, what is the need of this bullock cart sex? It is out of date.

Soon the day will come when children will not be born out of men's and women's sex – because we have suffered very much: blind children, retarded children, who have to live their life in utter agony and suffering because there were no means to clear up the situation. But now we have the means. Now love can be completely fun, a joy, a celebration. There is no responsibility, no fear of making the woman pregnant, because that keeps her in bondage; because you are a partner in creating a child, now you have to be a partner in bringing him up.

Man's past history has been really not human. It can be human only if the woman and the man are no longer just sex partners. That drags them both to the very lowest spaces. If they can love each other with respect, not using each other as commodities, men and women both will have a great uprising in consciousness.

The more your sex energy becomes love, the more you are a spiritual being.

Sex is only a reproductive process forced on you by nature. Nature has been using you just like a factory. And you don't even have the dignity to declare that "I am not a factory!" This can happen only if you are alert, aware, conscious of what you are doing, what you are thinking, how you are behaving; and that brings such grace and such beauty that the concern with physical beauty simply disappears.

I have seen many beautiful women with very ugly minds. I

have seen many beautiful men, but their beauty is not more than skin-deep. And this is the trouble: beauty is always skin-deep and ugliness goes to the very bones. Go on digging and you will find it, it is there: to the bones, to the marrow.

Love is the alchemy that can change that ugliness from within. And once it disappears from within, even an ordinary face, a homely face, starts shining with the bliss and joy of the beyond.

The Great Pilgrimage, Session 8, September 10, 1987

# Natural
# is Beautiful

JUST TODAY I was informed that billions of dollars are spent on plastic surgery in America alone. Almost half a million people every year are going through plastic surgery. In the beginning the age group that used to go through plastic surgery was when a woman – and it was confined only to women – when a woman started feeling old. She used to go through plastic surgery to remain a little younger, attractive for a few days more.

But a recent development is that the major part of the people who are going in for plastic surgery in America are men, not women, because now *they* want to be younger a little longer. Deep down they will become older, but their skin will show the tightness of a young man. And the most surprising thing in the report was that even a twenty-three-year-old boy has gone through plastic surgery to look younger. America is certainly the land of lunatics. Now if a twenty-three-year-old boy thinks that he needs to look younger...

It is so ugly to go against nature. It is so beautiful to be in tune with nature and whatever gift it brings: childhood or youth or old age. If your acceptance and your welcoming heart are ready, everything that nature brings has a beauty of its own.

According to my understanding – and all the Eastern seers are behind me in support – man becomes really beautiful and graceful at the highest point of his age, when all the foolishness of youth has gone; when all the ignorance of childhood has disappeared; when one has transcended the whole world of mundane experiences and has reached to a point where one can be a witness on the hills – while the whole world is moving down in the dark dismal valleys, blindly groping. The idea of remaining continuously young is also ugly. The whole world should be made aware that by forcing yourself to be young, you simply become more tense. You will never become relaxed.

And if plastic surgery is going to succeed, as it becomes a bigger and bigger profession in the world, then you will find a strange thing happening: everybody will start looking alike. Everybody will have the same size nose which is decided by computers; everybody has the same kind of face, the same cut. It will not be a beautiful world; it will lose all its variety, it will lose all its beautiful differences. People will become almost like machines, all alike, coming from the assembly line, Ford cars, one by one. They say that every minute one car comes out of the Ford factory similar to the one following it – in one hour, sixty cars. Twenty-four hours a day it goes on; the shifts of workers go on changing, but the assembly line goes on producing the same cars.

Do you want humanity also to be streamlined, assembled in a factory, exactly like everybody else, so that wherever you go you meet Sophia Loren? It would be very boring.

Everybody wants to live long, but no one wants to be old.

Why? – because of the next stage. Nobody is really afraid of old age, but after old age is death and nothing else. So everybody would like to live as long as possible, but never to become old, because to become old means you have entered into the area of death. Deep down the fear of becoming old is a fear of death, and only those who don't know how to live are afraid of death.

Youth is a malady of which one becomes cured a little every day. Old age is the cure. You have passed through the whole fire test of life, and you have come to the point where you can be utterly detached, aloof, indifferent.

But the West has never understood the beauty of old age. I can understand, but I cannot agree. In the West the idea is: the trouble with life is that there are so many beautiful women – and so little time. That's why nobody wants to become old, just to stretch the time a little more. But I say unto you: the trouble would be even worse if there was so much time and so few women! As it is, it is a perfect world.

The Great Pilgrimage, Session 19, September 28, 1987

# A New Beginning

## Osho,

*Something feels drastically wrong about the way society looks after – or fails to look after – the elderly. What can be done for those who are not physically or mentally incapacitated, but are retired from their professions and whose families have grown up?*

The problem of the elderly has arisen because man is living longer than he used to live before. All the old skeletons found in India, in China and other ancient countries, prove one thing: that nobody used to live more than forty years; hence the problem of the elderly never arose in those societies. It is because of this fact that the scriptures go on saying that in our country people never became old. It was not something great, it was simply that before old age they were dead. Death came before old age; now it comes after.

As a country becomes more advanced, people live longer – ninety years, a hundred years. In a few countries there are thousands of people who have crossed the boundary line of one hundred and fifty. And in a few special places – because of their food, their climate and their genetics – a few people have reached the age of one hundred and eighty, and they are still young; they are working just like anybody else.

But the problem for society is that employment is limited. The population growth is tremendous – new people are coming in such great numbers that we have to create places for them, we have to retire people. And as time passes we will have to retire people even earlier than we are retiring them now. Now in a few countries it is sixty years, in a few countries fifty-five years, but soon this will not be possible. People will have to retire by the age of around forty-five, because the pressure of the new people coming will be so great that if you don't give them opportunities they will create chaos.

But to retire somebody at the age of forty-five is dangerous, it creates many psychological problems. First, a person needs some work, some creativity, to feel that he is needed. This is one of the most essential psychological needs of man – to be needed. The moment you feel you are no longer needed, suddenly something starts dying within you, shrinking within you – as if the will to live has lost all its power, energy, hope. Tomorrow is nothing but darkness.

And the person who has become useless to the society...that's what retirement is. We make it as beautiful as we can by giving him a beautiful pocket watch, celebrating it – it is just a cover-up. The reality is, we are throwing the people in the junkyard: "You are no longer needed, your work is finished. Now, younger people, more educated, who know the latest scientific developments, are going to replace you. You are out of date."

Suddenly you have become a posthumous person. You will go on living, breathing, eating, but it will be just like an appendix in a book. The book is finished, and nobody reads the appendix. One starts losing dignity, self-respect; one starts feeling out of place everywhere. One is no longer connected with society, with the people who are now in power; a great gap has arisen.

These people are going through a tremendous inner turmoil, a crisis. To keep them in the family – as has always been done in the past – is to create a nuisance for the new ones, because these people have nothing to do except criticize. They are ready to get angry, easily annoyed, irritated, ready to fight. In fact these are their ways of making the society and the family feel that they are alive, that you cannot just ignore them. They are doing it in the wrong way, but whatever they are doing should be understood with great compassion: they are simply asking for a little attention. For their whole life they have been paid attention to – in the office, in the shop, in the government, wherever they were they were somebody. And now they are nobody, not even to their own children.

And the problem becomes more complex because the children

have no obligation to be bothered with these old people. They have a small life span of their own; soon they will be retired. Before retirement they want to enjoy life – to eat, drink and be merry. And these old people are sitting there, continuously watching what you are doing; they suddenly become very spiritual, moralistic disciplinarians; they start finding fault with everybody's life – and nobody likes it. Nobody wants to be interfered with. Their independence to live their life in their own way is their birthright.

And these old people – to the younger generation – look like idiots, for the simple reason that the younger generation knows more, it is better educated. Science is progressing in leaps and bounds. Every generation comes with the latest developments, canceling all old knowledge as false, as mistaken.

It was not so in the past. Things have changed so dramatically that unless we take the whole into account, we will not be able to solve the problem. In the past the situation was totally different, diametrically different. There was no gap between the younger and the older generations.

The gap has only been created in this century. In the past, by the time he was six or seven the young child would start following his father. If the father was a carpenter, he would start carrying his wood, his instruments. If the father was a woodcutter, he would go with him to the forest – whatever small help he could give, and whatever small amount he could learn...because profession came by birth. You were going to do the same thing your father did and your forefathers had been doing for centuries, there was no mobility. It was not that a shoemaker's son would become a carpenter, or a carpenter's son would become a goldsmith – the profession came by birth. So from the very beginning the child knew what he was going to become: he was going to become exactly a replica of his father.

The question of a gap did not arise. The father always knew more, and the child always knew less – because the only way of knowing was by experience. A carpenter's son had to learn by doing carpentry. Naturally the father was much more knowledgeable about the art, the craftsmanship, and at no time could the son say, "You are out of date."

This is why all the old civilizations respected old people, because the old people always knew more than the young people. Old people expect the same today also, but it is not possible –

they have forgotten that the basic root was that the older knew more than the younger.

Now the situation is just the reverse: the younger know more than the older.

Your father may have come out of the university thirty years ago. In thirty years, everything has changed. And when you come out of the university, the father cannot expect – *should* not expect – the same respect that was always given to him in the past. The situation is completely reversed. Now the son knows more; the father has to ask the son for his advice, because he is coming fresh from the university, bringing the latest research on any subject.

Now, experience is not the only way of learning. We have created schools, colleges, universities – an alternative way of learning, far quicker.

The way of experience is slower. Now, how quickly you can learn depends on your intelligence. Libraries are available, books are available, teachers are available. If you are only ready to learn, you can learn so much by the time you come out of the university that it is natural at many points to think: "My father is behaving stupidly, my father is doing things which are out of date – they should not be done."

Your father may be a doctor; he is giving medicines which you know – because you have come from the university – have been abandoned. They are not to be given, they are dangerous, and he is still prescribing them because in *his* time he learned that those were the right medicines. Such drastic changes have happened; the younger generation has come for the first time to a higher level of knowledge than the older. If he is considerate, a young person may respect old age – but it is going to be just formal, not real. In the past it was a real phenomenon, not formal – he really felt it. Now he cannot feel it.

And the rate of research in all subjects is such that now big books – particularly in physics, in chemistry, in biochemistry – are not written, because by the time you write a big book of a thousand pages most of it will have been proven wrong. So only periodicals, papers, are published, and in that too you have to be very quick because you are not working on the subject alone.

Albert Einstein was asked once, "If you had not discovered the theory of relativity, do you think it would have ever been discovered?"

He said, "Within three weeks – at the most."

It was very shocking, because people thought that there was only one Albert Einstein. He said, "That is true, but there are many like Albert Einstein around the world who are working along the same lines. It is only a question of who comes first, it is a race." It was found that another German physicist had already discovered everything about the theory of relativity, but he was late in publishing his paper; otherwise, Albert Einstein would not have been the first man to bring light to the whole subject. This man had discovered everything, he was just a little lazy about writing the paper – but his discovery was earlier than Albert Einstein's.

People are researching small details, not big subjects, because big subjects take a longer time. People are taking very small pieces of subjects so that they can finish them quickly before anybody else does, and then they can give the paper to the university or to whoever publishes the paper. Now there are thousands of universities around the world working on the same subjects, and thousands of scholars.

Today, every young person coming from the university is ahead of the older generation. His lifestyle has changed, his thinking about the world has changed, his values have changed – and the old people are constantly poking their noses into it.

So the only way that has been found is to put these old people in houses for the old. Out of duty, out of guilt, the children go to meet their parents there, but not for love, not for joy. And most often they are neglected; nobody ever goes there. Their lives are certainly very miserable.

They have lost their jobs, and with their jobs their respect; with their jobs their worth, with their jobs the feeling that they are somebody. Their ego is punctured. They have lost their family. Their children are grown up and don't want to live with them; they would like their children to listen to the music of Mozart, and the children are interested in the Beatles. The old people think, "Beatles? – this is not music. This is simply madness, this is not dance!" The gap is so big that it is unbridgeable.

This solution is sad. The children are gone, the family is gone. These old people's homes look sad; they seem to be waiting rooms for the graveyard – dull, depressed, dark.

Certainly there is a great problem, and this problem is going to become bigger every day.

My suggestion is: first, the moment old people retire and their families send them to the homes for the old, their marriages should also be canceled – because love can bring a new spring again. It doesn't matter whether you are fifty or sixty. They have produced children, they have lived together, now it is time...! They are departing from the family, they have departed from the job, they should depart from the marriage also – because their sadness has much to do with the situation of the husband and wife left alone. No friends, no children, no job – and they are tired of each other, they don't seem to take any interest in each other.

It should be optional: if some couple wants to live together, that is up to them, but if couples want to separate they should be respectfully separated so they can start their lives anew – and for the first time without worries. They have their pensions, money is no longer a problem; they can find new partners, new lovers.

And it has been psychologically established that if even an old man falls in love with a woman, his life is lengthened by at least ten years – because love gives juice to your roots. You become young again; you start looking at flowers again, thinking of poetry, thinking of painting, writing love letters.

So the first thing is that love should be given another chance. What is the harm? – if you can have two springs in your life... And now you are more experienced. You will not produce children again; that phase is over, you have tortured yourself enough. You will take every care that children are not produced.

It is a strange phenomenon: the moment somebody falls in love, many things change – his face has a different glow, his eyes become more shiny, he smiles more. He may go and dye his hair, get a beautiful set of teeth. He has to become a little younger – life is making a new beginning. To me, love is a kind of chemistry – it *is* chemistry. Your body starts functioning in a different way. He will start thinking, if he is a man, about going for morning walks, jogging, swimming, to keep his body fit, because now there is a woman.... And the woman is going to take care of her body at least twenty times more...

It will be a beautiful place, because then in those old people's homes people will paint their rooms in brighter colors, not dark and sad, gloomy. They will bring flowers, they will start gardening, may go for a world tour, may go for a long trip in a boat. Life can be a joy. They can meditate, they can study. Much that they always wanted to do and had no time to do...now they have time, they have money. They can paint, they can sculpt.

My own idea is that special classes should be opened in every university for these old people who want to learn painting, who want to learn sculpture, who want to learn music, who want to learn dancing. They should enter the university again – a second phase of education.

I have always had the idea that the first phase of education is the preparation for life and the second phase of education should be the preparation for death.

You don't have any preparation for death, no education for death. This is a lopsided situation. A person has lived half his life, and you trained him, educated him. Now the other half should not be left barren like a desert. He should begin again, with the second part of his education. He meditates, he learns creative arts, he dances, he writes poetry, novels.

Whatever he wanted to do in life...now life has respectfully given him time to do everything that has been just a desire in his mind, just a dream. Now it can be turned into a reality. And he should be freed from all old bondages...marriage, or any other kind of bondage – so he can start new adventures in every direction.

We can make the second part so beautiful that people who are still in the first part will feel jealous, will feel, "How long will it take for me to be retired? – because those old guys are really enjoying it. We are working, earning; they are simply relaxing, taking sun-baths on different beaches around the world, with different women."

The old people have to defeat the young – there is no need for *them* to be defeated. Right now they have taken a very defeatist attitude. They should take it as a challenge: "Now we will prove that old age is not a misery, that it can become a tremendously beautiful experience."

In fact, it has to be more beautiful than the first phase, because the first phase was only a preparation for the second:

And the second is the preparation for the eternal.

Sermons in Stones, Session 3, November 7, 1987

# Nothing Ends

AN ANCIENT TREE just by the side of my house has been dancing in the rain, and its old leaves are falling with such grace and beauty. Not only is the tree dancing in the rain and the wind, the old leaves leaving the tree are also dancing. There is celebration.

In the whole of existence nobody suffers from old age except man. In fact existence knows nothing about old age. It knows about ripening, it knows about maturing, it knows there is a time to dance, to live as intensely and as totally as possible, and there is a time to rest.

Those old leaves of the almond tree by the side of my house are not dying; they are simply going to rest, melting and merging into the same earth from which they have arisen. There is no sadness, no mourning, but an immense peace falling into rest in eternity. Perhaps another day, another time, they may be back again in some other form, on some other tree. They will dance again, they will sing again; they will rejoice with the moment.

Existence knows only a circular change: from birth to death, from death to birth, and it is an eternal process. Every birth implies death and every death implies birth. Every birth is preceded by a death and every death is succeeded by a birth. Hence existence is not afraid.

There is no fear anywhere, except in the mind of man.

Man seems to be the only sick species in the whole cosmos. Why all this sickness? It really should have been otherwise. Man should have enjoyed more, lived more each moment, whether it was in childhood or in youth or in old age, whether it was in birth or in death – it does not matter at all. You are transcendental to all these small episodes.

Thousands of births have happened to you and thousands of deaths, and those who can see clearly, they can understand it even more deeply, as if it is happening every moment. Something in you dies every moment and something in you is born anew. Life and death are not so separate, not separated by seventy years. Life and death are just like two wings of a bird, simultaneously happening; neither can life exist without death nor can death exist without life. Obviously they are not opposites, obviously they are complementaries. They need each other for their existence, they are interdependent; they are part of one cosmic whole.

But man is so unaware, so asleep that he is incapable of seeing a simple and obvious fact. Just a little awareness, not much, and you can see you are changing every moment; and change means something is dying, something is being reborn. Then birth and death become one; then childhood and its innocence becomes one with old age and its innocence. There is a difference, yet there is no opposition.

The child's innocence is really poor because it is almost synonymous with ignorance. The old man, ripe in age, who has passed through all the experiences of darkness and light, of love and hate, of joy and misery, who has been matured through life in different situations, has come to a point where he is no longer a participant in any experience. Misery comes, he watches; and happiness comes and he watches. He has become a watcher on the hill. Everything passes down in the dark valleys, but he remains on the sunlit peak of the mountain, simply watching in utter silence.

The innocence of old age is rich. It is rich in experience; it is rich in failures, in successes; it is rich in right actions, in wrong actions; it is rich in all the failures, in all the successes – it is rich multidimensionally. Its innocence cannot be synonymous with ignorance; its innocence can only be synonymous with wisdom.

Both are innocent, the child and the old man. But their innocences have a qualitative change, a qualitative difference. The child is innocent because he has not entered yet into the dark night of the soul. The old man is innocent – he has come out of the tunnel. One is going to suffer much; one has already suffered enough. One cannot avoid the hell that is ahead of him; the other has left the hell behind him.

In existence nothing begins and nothing ends. Just look all around...the evening is not the end, neither the morning is the beginning. The morning is moving towards the evening, and the evening is moving towards the morning. Everything is simply moving into different forms. There is no beginning and there is no end.

Why should it be otherwise with man? Man is not an exception. In this idea of being exceptional, of being special, different from the other animals and the trees and the birds, man has created his own hell, his paranoia. The idea that we are exceptional beings, we are human beings, has created a rift between you and existence. That rift causes all your fears and your misery, causes unnecessary anguish and angst in you.

And all your so-called leaders, whether religious or political or social, have all emphasized the rift; they have widened it. There has not been a single effort in the whole history of man to bridge the rift, to bring man back to the earth; to bring him back with the animals and with the birds and with the trees, and to declare an absolute unity with existence.

That is the truth of our being. Once it is understood you are neither worried about old age nor worried about death...because looking around, you can be absolutely satisfied that nothing ever begins – it has always been there – and nothing ever ends; it will remain always there.

The idea of being old fills you with great anxiety. It means now your days of life, of love, of rejoicing, are over; that now you will exist only in name. It will not be a rejoicing but only a dragging towards the grave.

Obviously you cannot enjoy the idea that you are just a burden on existence, just standing in a queue which is moving every moment towards the graveyard.

It is one of the greatest failures of all cultures and all civilizations in the world that they have not been able to provide a meaningful life, a creative existence for their old; that they have not been able to provide a beauty and grace, not only to old age, but to death itself.

You need not be worried about old age. It is your maturity; you have simply passed through every experience. You have grown so experienced that now you need not repeat those experiences again and again. This is transcendence.

You should rejoice, and I would like the whole world to understand the rejoicing: that it is our birthright to accept with deep gratitude old age and the final consummation of old age into death. If you are not graceful about it, if you cannot laugh at it, if you cannot disappear into the eternal leaving a laughter behind, you have not lived rightly; you have been dominated and directed by wrong people. They may have been your prophets, your messiahs, your saviors, your *tirthankaras,* they may have been your incarnations of gods, but they have all been criminals in the sense that they have deprived you of life and they have filled your hearts with fear.

My effort is to fill your heart with laughter. Each fiber of your being should love to dance in every situation, whether it is day or night, whether you are down or up. Irrespective of the situation, an undercurrent of cheerfulness should continue. This is authentic religiousness to me.

A few *sutras:*

An ancient man is one who wears his glasses in bed so he can get a better look at the girls he dreams about.

An ancient man is one who only flirts with young girls at parties so his wife will take him home.

The beauty of being ancient is that since you are too old to set a bad example, you can start giving good advice.

Only a really old man, well-versed in the wisdom of life, can say, "Puppy love is lots of fun but few men realize it is the beginning of a dog's life."

The Great Pilgrimage, Session 20, September 29, 1987

# Horizontal or Vertical

## Osho,

*I also am getting old.*
*Would you tell me a few laws of middle age?*

Everybody is getting old. The day you were born – since then you have been getting old, each moment, each day. Childhood is a flux, so is youth; only old age never evolves into something else, because life terminates. That is the unique quality of old age, that it brings you to ultimate rest.

As far as I am concerned I have never been a child, never a youth, will never become old and never will die. I know only one thing in me – and that is absolutely unchanging and eternal. But just for your sake...

There are many laws about middle age, because all over the world people become old, and many thinkers have been thinking, "What is this old age?" The first law is De Never's Last Law – obviously about old age, the law can also be the last: "Never speculate on that which can be known for certain." You know perfectly well you are getting old; now don't speculate on that – that will make you more miserable. This law is beautiful: "Never speculate on that which can be known for certain." In fact, in life, except for death, nothing is certain. Everything can be speculated upon, but not death; and old age is just the door to death.

"Middle age is when you begin to exchange your emotions for symptoms."

Lendel's Law: "You know you are getting old when a girl says 'No' and all you feel is relief."

"Old age is when you start to turn out the lights for economical rather than romantic reasons."

"Old age is that period of life when your idea of getting ahead is staying even."

"Old age is when you can do just as much as ever, but would rather not."

Old age is a mysterious experience, but all those laws have been found by the Western mind. I have not been able to discover anybody in the whole literature of the East who talks about old age. On the contrary, old age has been praised immensely, because in the East it has been thought that you are not old if your life has simply moved along a horizontal line; you are only aged. But if your life, your consciousness, has moved vertically, upwards, then you have attained the beauty, the glory of old age. Old age in the East has been synonymous with wisdom.

But man can go...these are the two paths. One is horizontal, from childhood to youth, to old age, and to death; and another is vertical, from childhood to youth, to old age, and to immortality. The difference of quality between these dimensions is immense, incalculable. The man who simply becomes a young man, then old, then dead, has remained identified with his body. He has not known anything about his being, because being is never born and never dies. It is always, it has been always, it is the whole of eternity.

On the vertical line, the child becomes a youth; but youth on the vertical line will be different than youth on the horizontal line. Childhood is innocent, but that is the point from where these two different dimensions separate. On the horizontal line youth is nothing but sensuality, sexuality and all kinds of other stupidities. On the vertical line youth is a search for truth, is a search for life – it is a longing to know oneself. A man on the vertical line cannot be called young if he is not meditative. And the same is true about old age.

On the horizontal line, old age is simply trembling, afraid of death. In old age one cannot think about anything except the graveyard and a darkness which goes on becoming darker and darker. One cannot conceive of oneself except as a skeleton. But on the vertical line, old age is a celebration: It is as beautiful as man has ever been – because youth is a little foolish, is bound to be, it is inexperienced. But old age has passed through all the experiences – good and bad, right and wrong – and has come to a state where it is no longer affected by anything concerned with body or mind. And it is a welcome. Old age on the vertical line is keeping its door open for the ultimate guest to come in. It is not an end, it is the beginning of a real life, of an authentic being. Hence, I continually make the distinction between growing old and growing up.

Very few people have been fortunate enough to grow up; the rest of humanity has only been growing old. Naturally they are all moving towards death. Only on the vertical line does death not exist. That is the way to immortality, to divinity.

Naturally, when a man becomes old in that dimension he has a grace and a beauty and a compassion and love. It has been noted again and again – there is a statement in Buddhist scriptures that as Buddha became older, he became more beautiful. This is a true miracle. This I call a true miracle, not walking on water, any drunkard can try this; not turning water into wine, every criminal can do that. This is a true miracle – Buddha became more beautiful than he was in his youth; he became more innocent than he was in his childhood. This is growth.

Unless you are moving on the vertical line, you are missing the whole opportunity of life. Here our whole effort is to block the horizontal line and open the blocked vertical line. Then every day you are coming closer to life, not farther away. Then your birth is not the beginning of death, your birth is the beginning of eternal life: just two different lines, and so much difference.

The West has never thought about it. The vertical line has never been mentioned, because they have not been brought up in a spiritual atmosphere where the real riches are inside you. Even if they think of God, they think of him as being outside. Gautam Buddha could deny God; I deny God – absolutely, there is no God – for the simple reason that we want you to turn inwards. If God is, or anything similar, it has to be found inside you; it has to be found in your own eternity, in your own ecstasy.

But to think oneself a body-mind structure is the most dangerous idea that has happened to people. That destroys their whole grace, their whole beauty. They are constantly trembling and afraid of death, and trying to keep old age as far away as possible.

In the West, if you say to an old woman, "You look so young," and she knows she is no longer young, she will stand before the mirror for hours to check whether any youth has remained anywhere. But she will not deny it; she will be immensely happy. In the East nobody says to an old woman, "You are young." On the contrary, old age is so respected, so loved, that to say to somebody "You look younger than your age," is a kind of insult.

I am reminded of one incident that happened in my life. I was staying in Changha – a far corner of Maharashtra – with a very rich family, and they were very much interested in an astrologer. They loved me. I used to go at least three times per year – that was their quota – and I used to stay there for at least three, four days each time. Once, when I went there, they had arranged with the astrologer to come and to look at my hands and tell things about me, without asking me. When I came to know about it everything was fixed, the astrologer was sitting in the sitting-room. So I said, "Okay, let us enjoy that too!"

I showed him my hand; he pondered over it and he said, "You must be at least eighty years old." Of course one of the daughters of the rich man freaked out, "This is stupid! What kind of astrology...?" because at that time I was not more than thirty-five. Even a blind man could have measured – thirty-five and eighty! She was really angry and she told me, "I am finished with this astrologer. What else can he know?" I said, "You don't understand. You are more Westernized, educated in the Western style, you have been to the West for your education, you can't understand what he was saying." She said, "What was he saying? It was so clear, there is no need to understand; he was simply showing his stupidity! A thirty-five-year-old man, and he is saying you are eighty years old." I said, "Be patient," and I told her a story about Emerson.

A man asked Emerson, "How old are you?" Emerson said, "Near about three hundred and sixty years." The man could not believe it – and he had always believed in Emerson, that he is a man of truth. What has happened – a slip of the tongue? Or has he become senile? Or is he joking? But to make things clear he said, "I did not hear what you said; just tell me, how old?" Emerson said, "You have heard – three hundred and sixty years." The man said, "I cannot believe it, you don't look more than sixty." Emerson said, "You are right in a way; on the vertical I am three hundred and sixty, and on the horizontal I am sixty."

Perhaps he is the first Western man to use this Eastern expression, of horizontal and vertical. He was immensely interested in the East, and he has a few glimpses which bring him closer to the seers of the *Upanishads*. He said, "Actually I have lived sixty years, you are right. But I have lived as much in sixty years as you will be able to live in even three hundred and sixty years. I have lived six times more."

The vertical line does not count years, it counts your experiences. And on the vertical line is the whole treasure of existence – not only immortality, not only a feeling of divineness, but the first experience of love without hate, the first experience of compassion, the first experience of meditation, the first experience with a tremendous explosion of enlightenment.

It is not a coincidence that in the West the word "enlightenment" does not have the same meaning as in the East. They say that after the Dark Ages came the Age of Enlightenment. People like Bertrand Russell, Jean-Paul Sartre, Jaspers – they call these very enlightened geniuses. They don't understand that they are misusing the word – degrading it into the mud. Neither Bertrand Russell is enlightened nor Jean-Paul Sartre nor Jaspers; enlightenment does not happen on the horizontal. Even in his old age Jean-Paul Sartre was still running after young girls. Bertrand Russell changed his wife so many times – and he lived long, on the horizontal, almost a century. But even in his old age his interests were as stupid as young people's.

The East understands that the word "enlightenment" has nothing to do with genius, has nothing to do with intelligence; it has something to do with discovering your real, authentic being. It is discovering God within you.

On the vertical line there is love, no law. There is the growing experience of becoming more and more spiritual and less and less physical, more and more meditative and less and less mind, more and more divine and less and less this trivial, material world in which we are so much enmeshed. On the vertical line, slowly you feel desires disappearing, sensuality disappearing, sexuality disappearing, ambitions disappearing, will to power disappearing, your slavery in all its aspects – religious, political, national – disappearing. You are becoming more an individual, and with your individuality growing clear and luminous, the whole of humanity is becoming one in your eyes – you cannot discriminate.

There are great experiences on the vertical line; on the horizontal line there is only decline. On the horizontal line the old man lives in the past. He thinks of those beautiful days, those Arabian nights when he was young. He thinks also of those beautiful days when there was no responsibility and he was a child running after butterflies. In fact his whole life he has been running after butterflies. Even in old age...

Mulla Nasruddin was passing along the street and he saw a beautiful young woman, so he gave her a good nudge. The woman was shocked, because Mulla was old; his hair was pure, silver white. The woman said, "You should be ashamed – your hair is pure white! You are the age of my grandfather – you should have been dead by now, and you are showing your ugliness." Mulla said, "Listen, my hair is white, that's true, but my heart is still black – pitch black!"

On the horizontal line that's what happens – your hair will become white, but you don't become white. In fact, on the contrary, as you grow old, you become more and more infatuated by desires because now you know ahead is only death, so enjoy as much as possible – although enjoying becomes difficult, physically you have lost the energy. So the old man on the horizontal line becomes cerebrally sexual – he is continuously thinking of sex.

Psychologists have been watching thousands of people, and they have concluded that every man thinks of a woman at least once in every three minutes. You just check it! That will show you on what line you are – horizontal or vertical. And each woman thinks of a man once in seven minutes. That is the difference that creates conflict; the moment the husband comes and asks, "Dear, what about it?" she says, "I have a headache...don't torture me any more." The difference is, she thinks of sex only one time in seven minutes – that means one day in seven days – and the man thinks of sex one time in three minutes. That is the average. In old age those three minutes shrink into one minute. The old man has nothing else to do but think – and what else is there to think about? He imagines beautiful women.

One day Mulla Nasruddin was sitting on his balcony watching the beautiful sunset, and suddenly he shouted to his servant, "Bring my glasses, bring my glasses quick!" The servant said, "What calamity has happened?" He brought his glasses. Mulla said, "You idiot, when I say quick it *means* quick. We missed the opportunity." The servant said, "I don't understand, what opportunity?" Mulla said, "Such a beautiful woman was going by, but my eyes can't figure out whether she is really beautiful or I am imagining. Glasses were needed, and by the time you brought the glasses, she was gone." The servant said, "You are under a wrong impression: it was not a woman, it is my brother who has come to see me. Nobody else has passed."

The old man is continuously thinking of the past. This is the psychology: the child thinks of the future because he has no past. There is no question of thinking of the past, no yesterday. He thinks of days to come, of the whole, long life; seventy years gives him space. He wants to become big enough quickly, to do the things that all big people are doing. The old man has no future – future means death. He does not want even to talk about the future. The future makes him tremble, the future means the grave. He talks about the past.

And the same is true about countries. For example, a country like India never thinks of the future. That means it has become old – it is symptomatic. It always thinks of the past. It always goes on playing the life of Rama and Sita; for centuries, the same story... Every village is making a drama. It always goes on thinking of Buddha and Mahavira and Adinatha and the *Rig Veda* and the *Upanishads*. Everything has passed, now the country is simply waiting to die; there is no future.

According to the Indian idea – and that is the idea of the old mentality, the mind of the old man – the best age was millions of years ago, it was called *Satyuga,* the Age of Truth. Then man started falling. You can see the psychological parallel; there are four ages – childhood, youth, middle age, old age. In the same way he has projected four ages for life itself. The first age is innocent, just like a child – very balanced. They give the example that it has, just like a table, four legs – perfectly balanced. And then the decline starts.

In India, the idea of evolution has never existed, but on the contrary just the opposite idea. The word is not even used in the West; you may not have even heard of the word, but that's what India has been thinking – it is *involution,* not evolution. We are shrinking, we are falling down. In the second stage of the fall one leg is lost – the table becomes a tripod. It is still balanced, but not as much as it was with four legs. In the third stage it loses another leg; now it is standing only on two legs, absolutely unbalanced. And this is the fourth stage – even two legs are not available, you are standing on one leg. How long can you stand?

The first stage is called Satyuga, the Age of Truth; the second is simply named by the number, *Treta* – the third, because only three legs are left. The third is called *Dwapar* – again only the number, *dwa;* moving through many other languages it becomes *twa,* and then finally it becomes two. And the fourth age they have called *Kaliyuga,* the Age of Darkness. We are living in the Age of Darkness.

This is the mind of the old man; ahead there is only darkness and nothing else. The child thinks of the future, of the golden future. The old man thinks of the golden past. But this happens only on the horizontal line. On the vertical line the past is golden, the present is golden, the future is golden – it is a life of tremendous celebration.

So rather than being worried about the laws of old age, think on which line your train is moving. There is still time to change trains; it is always time to change trains, because from every moment that bifurcation is available. You can shift, shift from the horizontal to the vertical – only that is important.

The Invitation, Session 27, September 4, 1987

# Growing Up

## Osho,

*I was fifty-six years old when I first came to you and realized what a wastage my life had been up till then, an increasing unreality. Now I am sixty-seven, and although I still feel youthful, I have to keep reminding myself that I am old so that I can accept it gracefully. So much of me still feels like a lost little girl, and when I look at your grace and beauty – ageless, young and old both together – I do not feel so sad.*

*Will you say something to me about old age?*

It is one of the most significant problems because the way we have lived up to now has been unnatural, unpsychological, unspiritual. It has created so many problems.

For example, age – a person can either grow old or grow up. The person who only grows old has not lived at all. He has passed time, but he has not lived. All his life is nothing but repression. I teach you not to grow old. That does not mean you will not become old, it means I give you another dimension: growing up. Certainly you will grow old, but that will only be as far as the body is concerned. Your consciousness, *you*, will not grow old; you will only grow up. You will go on growing in maturity.

But all the religions of the world have been committing such crimes that they cannot be forgiven. They have not been teaching you how to live, they have been teaching you how *not* to live – how to renounce life, how to renounce the world. This world, according to the religious, is a punishment; you are in jail. So the only thing is to try to escape from the jail as quickly as possible.

This is not true – life is not a punishment. Life is so valuable that it cannot be a punishment, it is a reward. And you should be thankful to existence that it has chosen you – to breathe through you, to love through you, to sing through you, to dance through you.

If one keeps growing up in maturity and understanding one never becomes old; one is always young because one is always learning. Learning keeps you young. One is always young because one is not burdened with repressions. And because one is weightless, one feels as if one is just a child – a newcomer to this beautiful earth.

I have heard that three priests were going to Pittsburg. They reached the window to purchase their tickets, and the woman at the window who was selling the tickets was extraordinarily beautiful. Her clothes were almost negligible – she had beautiful breasts – and with a plunging neckline.

The youngest of the priests went up to the window...but he had forgotten all about the journey, he was only seeing those beautiful breasts! The woman asked, "What can I do for you?"

He said, "Three tickets for Titsburg."

The woman freaked out. She said, "You are a priest!"

The second one pushed him aside and told the woman, "Don't get angry – he's just new, immature. You just give us three tickets for Titsburg."

The woman looked..."Are all these men mad or something?"

"And remember one thing: I would like to have the change in nipples and dimes."

Now the woman started shouting and screaming, "This is too much!"

The oldest priest came in and said, "My daughter, don't be angry. These fellows stay in the monastery; they don't come out, they don't see anything. You should have a little understanding about their life-they have renounced their life. Just sit down. Three tickets for Titsburg." The woman could not believe them – all three seemed to be idiots! And the old priest said, "Remember one thing, I admonish you: use better clothes to cover your beautiful body. Otherwise, remember, on the Judgment Day Saint Finger will point his peter at you!"

This is the situation of the obsessed person. The more you deny life, the more you become obsessed with the same life. Up to now we have not allowed man to have a non-obsessional life. All the religions and the governments are angry with me for the simple reason that I am in favor of you, your freedom and a non-obsessional life – a pure, natural flow, joyous, making the whole of life a paradise.

We are not searching for any paradise in the clouds. If it is there, we will get hold of it, but first we have to make a paradise here on the earth; that will be our preparation. If we can live in a paradise on the earth, then wherever paradise is, it is ours; nobody else can claim it – at least not these priests and monks and nuns! All these people are bound towards hell, because on the surface they are one thing and inside it is just the opposite.

Try to be natural. Risk everything to be natural and you will not be at a loss.

Sermons in Stones, Session 13, December 12, 1986

# Gracefully Surrendering the Things of Youth

*L*IFE TEACHES YOU everything that you need. Life is the only university. Take the counsel of the years very kindly, very understandingly. In fact, each day one has to surrender many things of yesterday; each day one has to die to the past. When you were a child you were so interested in toys, all kinds of toys. When you became a youth you renounced those toys. In fact, you did not deliberately renounce, you simply became a grown-up and they withered away from your mind, they disappeared.

Once it was so difficult to go to bed without your teddy bear. But learning is difficult: the teddy bear has disappeared – now it is very difficult to go to sleep without your wife or without your husband. Now the wife is the teddy bear of the husband! The child has his own ways; for example, he will cling to the blanket and then only can he go to sleep. Now you have to make love before you can go to sleep – just a replacement. But nothing has been learned; a new habit, a new substitute, but you are the same, childish person.

The child used to go to sleep only when the mother gave her breast to him; now you will play with the breasts of your wife. It is the same old foolishness! At least the child has some reason; you don't have any reason at all. Have you seen the silliness of it? Playing with the breasts of your woman, can't you see your silliness? What are you doing? The child has some reason – the breast is his nourishment. But you have not gone beyond it yet; you are still clinging to something – of course unconsciously.

Mrs. Glowicki was walking down the street with her right breast exposed. A man stopped her and with some embarrassment pointed it out. "Oh, my God," cried the Polish woman, "I left my baby on the bus!"

The child has some reason – it is his nourishment – but a grown-up person always looking at the breasts of women...or avoiding them, it is the same. If you are a monk you will avoid, but what are you avoiding? Whatsoever you are avoiding, you want to see. And women know it perfectly well, so they. go on pretending to have big breasts, getting artificial breasts, many artificial devices to make the breasts look young. The real breasts may be just hanging down touching their belly buttons, but fools are deceived.

Only on the surface do you become a young man or a young woman; deep down the child is still trying to live. One becomes old, but youth persists psychologically. It is very rare to find an old man – and wise. You can find many dirty old men, but old men *and* wise – very difficult, because the first necessity for wisdom is renouncing the past. Every day it has to be renounced; that is the counsel of the years...gracefully to surrender the things of the past.

When you are a young man, surrender the things of your childhood. When you are old, surrender the things of your youth. Go on surrendering gracefully – and remember the word "gracefully." Don't escape, don't run, don't avoid, don't close your eyes. That is not grace. That simply shows you are as ignorant as ever, just pretending to be holy.

"Gracefully" .means through understanding, through real growing. Growing in age is not growing up; that is only aging. Growing up happens only when you go on renouncing the past every day, every moment, really. Each moment die to the past that is no more. Come out of it so you can remain fresh, so you can remain clean, so you can remain clear. Only that clarity can encounter the ultimate truth.

Guida Spirituale, Session 9, September 3, 1980

# The Beauty of It!

*E*VERYBODY IS SOONER or later bound to become old. We have to understand the beauty of old age, and we have to understand the freedom of old age. We have to understand the wisdom of old age; we have to understand its tremendous detachment from all the foolish things that go on in the lives of people who are still young.

Old age gives you a height, and if this height can be joined with meditation...you will wonder: why did you waste your youth? why did your parents destroy your childhood? why was not meditation given to you as the first gift, the day you were born? But whenever you get it, it is still not too late. Even just a few moments before your death, if you can get the meaning of your being, your life has not been a wastage.

Old age in the East has been immensely respected. In the past it was thought almost a shameless act – when your children are getting married, when your children are giving birth to children... and you are still infatuated, you are still in the bondage of biology. You should rise; this is the time to leave the ground for other fools to play football. At the most you can be a referee, but not a player...

Unless you accept everything that life brings you with gratefulness, you are missing the point. Childhood was beautiful; youth has its own flowers; old age has its own peaks of consciousness. But the trouble is that childhood comes on its own; for old age you have to be very creative.

Old age is your own creation.

It can be a misery, it can be a celebration; it can simply be a despair and it can also be a dance. It all depends how deeply ready you are to accept existence, whatsoever it brings. One day it will bring death too – accept it with gratitude.

The Great Pilgrimage, Session 13, September 12, 1987

# PART TWO

# A Joke

THE OLD BOSS had managed to get a date with his secretary, but was worried about his diminished potency; so he went to the doctor and asked for something to pep him up. The doctor gave him two pills and said, "Take these with your dinner tonight and you should not have any trouble performing later on."

So the old man and his date went to a beautiful restaurant, and when they had ordered their soup the old man took the waiter aside and asked him to put the two pills into his soup before he served it.

They waited for twenty minutes, and still the waiter had not brought their soup. So the old man angrily called the waiter over and said, "What the hell has happened to the soup?"

"I'm sorry, sir," said the waiter, "but I did what you ordered and put those pills in your soup, and now I'm just waiting for the noodles to lie down again!"

The Great Pilgrimage, Session 12, September 12, 1987

# A Few Maxims

REMEMBER: OLD AGE is when the candles cost more than the cake.

And also remember: Old age is when getting it up gets you down.

The eyes of the dead are closed gently; we also have to open gently the eyes of the living.

When you are up to your nose, keep your mouth shut.

And never forget that money can't buy happiness, but it can buy you the kind of misery you prefer. In old age certainly one wants to be happy, but nothing can buy happiness. In old age people have money, but money can buy only the misery you prefer, not happiness.

And this is a tremendously significant maxim to remember as far as old people are concerned: Whenever you feel the urge to exercise, just lie down and wait until it passes.

If you have really become old, just have a look at your passport. If you actually look like your passport photo, you are not well enough to travel.

The Invitation, Session 29, September 5, 1987

# Start Moving
# Upwards

## Osho,

*The prospect of joining the ranks of the sexually unemployed nearabout the age of forty-two has got me into very hot water with my beloved. She's wanting all manner of guarantees and assurances, and in writing! On the other hand, if I really do have nine more years to go, that will not only be the end of my sex life, but the end of me, full stop!*

You have only one misunderstanding in your question – the full stop. It is not a full stop, it is a semicolon.

Everything will continue but on a higher level, on a better level. The moment sex disappears it does not mean that you don't have life anymore, unless you have this wrong idea that sex and life are synonymous. They are not.

The moment sex starts disappearing, a great spiritual revolution starts happening in you. The same energy that was moving downwards starts moving upwards. It is the same energy that has brought you into the world. It is the same energy that can take you to the other world – called by different religions, different names – *nirvana, moksha,* paradise, the kingdom of God…just different names.

Sex energy is the only energy there is.

Either you can destroy it, spoil it, throw it away, or you can be more articulate, more wise, and transform it.

Guilt cannot be transformed because it is not part of your being, but sex can be transformed because you are made of nothing but sex energy; all the cells of your body are sexual cells.

The full stop never comes. It is always a comma or a semi-colon, but life goes on and on without any full stop.

Sermons in Stones, Session 28, September 19, 1987

# Live It and Finish with It

**W**HEN YOU GET tired of sex, fed up with it, then the same energy that was involved in sex can be used for meditation. But you can't have both together – that will be like riding on two horses together. Either you have sex or meditation.

One thing you have to understand, you cannot have meditation unless you have transcended sex. But transcendence should not be understood in the old way – as repression. Transcendence is experience – so much experience that you don't think any more of attraction, infatuation. Sex simply drops like dry leaves from the trees. It is not that you have to make an effort; if you have to make some effort to drop it, it will remain with you. And if it is there, meditation is impossible – it won't let you be silent.

Sex is one of the most torturous forms of biological slavery. It is good to get rid of it by experiencing it with totality and intensity – don't think of meditation at all. Sex lived totally will bring you to meditation; and then meditation will be very easy, because there will be no biological pull against it. Sex is absolutely the first, because that is your biological bondage – you have to get free of it. And the way to get free of it is not to fight with it. That's what religious people have been doing for centuries, and they have not succeeded; not a single person has succeeded in transcending sex by fighting it, by repressing it. Live it. And don't live it with guilt, don't live it as if it is something wrong, as if it is a sin. It is not.

From fourteen to twenty-one your sexual energy is at the highest peak – exactly between fourteen and twenty-one. That means seventeen-and-a-half is the climax of your sexual energy.

50

But this society has lived with such repressive and unnatural, unscientific, ideas that these are the years when you are told to be celibate. And these are the years when you could have lived sex, and celibacy would have come by itself by the time you were forty-two. Between twenty-one and twenty-eight, sex is very normal, very natural. From twenty-eight to thirty-five, sex starts declining. From thirty-five to forty-two sex reaches its ultimate decline. From forty-two to forty-nine sex disappears. That's why in ancient India the wise people had decided that by the time one is fifty, one should start preparing for *vanprast*. One's face should be now turned towards the mountains, towards the forest – that is the meaning of *vanprast*. One is still in the world, but now one's whole consciousness has turned and is getting ready to move into the deep forest to be alone; the days of meditation have come.

By the time a person is fifty his children will be near about twenty-five; they must be getting married, they must be getting into a profession. The father can look for twenty-five years more. These are the twenty-five years, from fifty to seventy-five, that he can watch – he can live in the world yet not be of the world. He can watch his children slowly taking over. And from seventy-five all his interest in the world has disappeared; then meditation will be his only interest.

But this is just a formal categorization. It depends on you and your intensity of living. You can be beyond sex by the time you are thirty-five, you can be beyond sex without much difficulty when you are forty-two. But it is unfortunate that people die still as foolish as young people. Psychologists have come to the conclusion that most people die with the idea of sex – that it is their last idea. They may be repeating the name of God, but inside they are thinking, "If it is possible...one more time!" They have not lived their life wholeheartedly. That's why something that should have ended at forty-two has continued up to eighty, up to ninety.

Live your first interest and be finished with it. But be finished with it by living it joyously – there is nothing wrong, there is no sin. And meditation will become absolutely simple and easy because your mind will not be burdened with sexual infatuation and desire. That is your only bondage; all other bondages are secondary, all other bondages are branches of your sexuality.

For what do you want money? For what do you want power? Have you watched, that all other interests are centered on sex? A man without money will not be able to get the most beautiful woman he wants. A man without power will not be able to get the most beautiful woman. All your so-called desires are all centered on a single fact, a single interest, and that is sex.

Just live it, and live it joyously without any fear of hell or heaven. There is no hell and no heaven. And once you are out of it, once sex has disappeared like smoke disappearing into the sky and you cannot see it, then meditation is so easy. You don't have to make any effort, you have just to sit silently with closed eyes, relaxed, and you will find meditation is there.

My suggestion to you: first sex, because it is more basic to your body, to your life – it is the foundation of life. Meditation is the highest peak, but sex is the roots; first think of the roots. Meditation is the flowers; they come at the very end, at the very top of the tree they will come. But don't try both together; otherwise you will remain wishy-washy, always half-hearted – meditating and thinking about sex, making love and thinking about Gautam Buddha! This will simply drive you crazy.

The Great Pilgrimage, Session 5, September 6, 1987

# *Your Aloneness*

## *Osho,*

*You said that we are born alone, we live alone and we die alone. Yet it seems as if from the day we are born, whatever we are doing, whoever we are, we seek to relate to others.*

*Would you please comment?*

The question that you have asked is the question of every human being.

We are born alone, we live alone, and we die alone.

Aloneness is our very nature.

But we are not aware of it.

Because we are not aware of it, we remain strangers to ourselves, and instead of seeing our aloneness as a tremendous beauty and bliss, silence and peace, at-easeness with existence, we misunderstand it as loneliness. Loneliness is a misunderstood aloneness. Once you misunderstand your aloneness as loneliness, the whole context changes. Aloneness has a beauty and grandeur, a positivity; loneliness is poor, negative, dark, dismal.

Everybody is running away from loneliness. It is like a wound; it hurts. To escape from it, the only way is to be in a crowd, to become part of a society, to have friends, to create a family, to have husbands and wives, to have children. In this crowd, the basic effort is that you will be able to forget your loneliness. But nobody has ever succeeded in forgetting it. That which is natural to you, you can try to ignore, but you cannot forget it; it will assert itself again and again.

And the problem becomes more complex because you have

never seen it as it is; you have taken it for granted that you are born lonely.

The dictionary meaning is the same – that shows the mind of the people who create dictionaries. They don't understand at all the vast difference between loneliness and aloneness. Loneliness is a gap. Something is missing, something is needed to fill it, and nothing can ever fill it because it is a misunderstanding in the first place. As you grow older, the gap also grows bigger.

People are so afraid to be by themselves that they do any kind of stupid thing. I have seen people playing cards alone; the other party is not there. They have invented games in which the same person plays cards from both sides. Somehow one wants to remain engaged. That engagement may be with people, may be with work.... There are workaholics; they are afraid when the weekend comes close – what are they going to do? And if they don't do anything, they are left to themselves, and that is the most painful experience.

You will be surprised to know that it is on the weekends that most of the accidents in the world happen. People are rushing in their cars to resort places, to sea beaches, to hill stations – bumper to bumper. It may take eight hours, ten hours to reach, and there is nothing for them to do because the whole crowd has come with them. Now their house, their neighborhood, their city is more peaceful than this sea resort. Everybody has come. But *some* engagement...

People are playing cards, chess; people are watching television for hours – the average American watches television five hours a day. People are listening to the radio...just to avoid themselves. For all these activities, the only reason is not to be left alone; it is very fearful. And this idea is taken from others. Who has told you that to be alone is a fearful state? Those who have known aloneness say something absolutely different. They say there is nothing more beautiful, more peaceful, more joyful than being alone.

But you listen to the crowd. The people who live in misunderstanding are in such a majority, that who bothers about a Zarathustra or a Gautam Buddha? These single individuals can be wrong, can be hallucinating, can be deceiving themselves or deceiving you, but millions of people cannot be wrong. And millions of people agree that to be left to oneself is the worst experience in life; it is hell.

But any relationship that is created because of the fear, because of the inner hell of being left alone, cannot be satisfying. Its very root is poisoned. You don't love your woman, you are simply using her not to be lonely. Neither does she love you, she is also in the same paranoia; she is using you not to be left alone. Naturally, in the name of love anything may happen – except love. Fights may happen, arguments may happen, but even they are preferred to being lonely: at least somebody is there and you are engaged, you can forget your loneliness. But love is not possible, because there is no basic foundation for love.

Love never grows out of fear.

You are asking, "You said the other day that we are born alone, we live alone and we die alone. Yet it seems as if from the day we are born, whatever we are doing, whoever we are, we seek to relate to others."

This seeking to relate to others is nothing but escapism.

This whole effort – whether of relationships or remaining busy in a thousand and one things – is just to escape from the idea that you are lonely. And I want it to be emphatically clear to you that this is where the meditator and the ordinary man part.

The ordinary man goes on trying to forget his loneliness, and the meditator starts getting more and more acquainted with his aloneness. He has left the world; he has gone to the caves, to the mountains, to the forest, just for the sake of being alone. He wants to know who he is. In the crowd it is difficult; there are so many disturbances. And those who have known their aloneness have known the greatest blissfulness possible to human beings – because your very being is blissful.

After being in tune with your aloneness, you can relate; then your relationship will bring great joys to you because it is not out of fear. Finding your aloneness you can create, you can be involved in as many things as you want, because this involvement will not anymore be running away from yourself. Now it will be your expression; now it will be the manifestation of all that is your potential.

Only such a man – whether he lives alone or lives in the society, whether he marries or lives unmarried makes no difference – is always blissful, peaceful, silent. His life is a dance, is a song, is a flowering, is a fragrance. Whatever he does, he brings his fragrance to it.

But the first basic thing is to know your aloneness absolutely.

This escape from yourself you have learned from the crowd.

Because everybody is escaping, you start escaping. Every child is born in a crowd and starts imitating people; what others are doing, he starts doing. He falls into the same miserable situations as others are in, and he starts thinking that this is what life is all about. And he has missed life completely.

So I remind you, don't misunderstand aloneness as loneliness. Loneliness is certainly sick; aloneness is perfect health.

Ginsberg visits Doctor Goldberg. "Ja, you are sick," Goldberg tells him.

"Not good enough. I want another opinion," says Ginsberg.

"Okay," said Doctor Goldberg, "you are ugly too."

We are all committing the same kinds of misunderstandings continually.

I would like my people to know that your first and most primary step towards finding the meaning and significance of life is to enter into your aloneness. It is your temple; it is where your God lives. And you cannot find this temple anywhere else: you can go on to the moon, to Mars...

Once you have entered your innermost core of being, you cannot believe your own eyes: you were carrying so much joy, so many blessings, so much love...and you were escaping from your own treasures.

Knowing these treasures and their inexhaustibility, you can move now into relationships, into creativity. You will help people by sharing your love, not by using them. You will give dignity to people by your love; you will not destroy their respect. And you will, without any effort, become a source for them to find their own treasures too. Whatever you make, whatever you do, you will spread your silence, your peace, your blessings into everything possible.

But this basic thing is not taught by any family, by any society, by any university. People go on living in misery, and it is taken for granted. Everybody is miserable, so it is nothing much if you are miserable; you cannot be an exception.

But I say unto you: You can be an exception. You just have not made the right effort.

The Golden Future, Session 6, April 25, 1987

# PART THREE

# Becoming Free

## Osho,

*I am sixty-two and young people accept me as one of them. How is this possible?*

Meditation is a transformation of your whole being. You are no more part of a crowd, no more a cog in the wheel. You have taken your responsibility on your own shoulders; you have become a free individual.

Nationality will disappear, because these are all arbitrary lines, man-made – and their existence is ugly, because their existence shows that man is not yet mature; otherwise, what is the need to have so many nations, and every nation having great armies?

People are dying in poverty, and seventy percent of the national income all over the world goes to the military. Humanity is living on only thirty percent, and the army gets everything else – naturally, because they have sold their lives and they are being prepared for death, either to kill or be killed.

This seems so useless. Why should there be wars? Why should there be violence? And why should nations, after five thousand years of experience, continue to show that they are cancerous, destructive?

The man of meditation is bound to be a citizen of the world. He is not going to be a Christian or a Hindu or a Mohammedan because he can contact existence himself; there is no need of any mediator, no need of any priest, holy book, church. All these religions have been creating nothing but bloodshed, burning living human beings and doing all kinds of ugly acts against innocent humanity. As you become more silent, as your eyes become more clear, as the smoke that surrounds you disappears, then religions, nations, discriminations between black and white, discriminations between men and women – all are going to disappear.

It is right you are feeling ageless.

Meditation starts taking you beyond time because it is going to take you beyond death.

You will be surprised that in Sanskrit there is only one word for both death and time. It is *kal. Kal* also means tomorrow – tomorrow there is only death and nothing else; life is today.

As you become more peaceful... Your tensions are your weight. When the tensions are not there, you become weightless. And the consciousness which is your reality has no time-space limitation. Your body grows from childhood, to youth, to old age, to death – these changes are happening only to the body. These are changing the furniture in the house – painting the house, changing its architecture-but the man who lives in the house, the master of the house, is unaffected by all these things.

Consciousness is the master.

Your body is only the house.

So the moment you enter meditation you have touched within yourself something of the universal – which has no age, which has no limitation either of time or space.

This is not only happening to you. I receive many letters from older sannyasins saying that they are feeling so young, and they don't see any generation gap. They mix with sannyasins and not for a moment does the idea come that they are eighty years old and these are twenty-year-old kids. But they communicate and nobody thinks that this is strange.

One woman sannyasin from Scotland wrote to me, "Now, Bhagwan it is going too far!" She is seventy-eight, and is now running after butterflies! The whole village thinks she has gone mad, because she is continuously laughing and enjoying and the village cannot believe it. Because they have seen her always miserable, they cannot believe what has happened to her. She is behaving like a small child.

She asked me, "What to do? Should I try to behave in the old way?"

I said to her, "You can try, but you cannot succeed. So don't waste your time, just go after the butterflies. And why bother about the idiots of the village? You enjoy yourself."

Meditation is not something mental:

Meditation is something concerned with your being.

Just plugging into it a little...and suddenly everything is different. The body will go its own way, but you will know you are not the body. People will die, but you will know that death is impossible. Your own death will come – but meditation prepares you for death so that you can go on dancing and singing into the ultimate silence, leaving the form behind and disappearing into the formless.

Sermons in Stones, Session 8, December 17, 1986

# *Meditation Is...*

 *M*EDITATION IS THE only contribution the East has made to humanity. The West has made many contributions – thousands of scientific inventions, immense progress in medicine, unbelievable discoveries in all the dimensions of life. But still, this single contribution of the East is far more valuable than all the contributions of the West.

The West has become rich, it has all the technology to be rich. The East has become poor, immensely poor, because it has not looked for anything else except for one thing, and that is one's own inner being. Its richness is something which cannot be seen, but it has known the highest peaks of bliss, the greatest depth of silence. It has known the eternity of life; it has known the most beautiful flowering of love, compassion, joy. Its whole genius has been devoted to a single search – you can call it ecstasy.

Meditation is only a technique to reach to the ecstatic state, to the state of divine intoxication. It is a simple technique, but the mind makes it very complex. Mind has to make meditation very complex and difficult because both cannot exist together. Meditation is the death of the mind; naturally, mind resists every effort for meditation. And it is clever and cunning enough to give you false directions and call them meditations.

Meditation starts by your being separate from the mind, by being a witness. That is the only way of separating yourself from anything. If you are looking at the light, naturally one thing is certain, you are not the light, you are one who is looking at it. If you are watching the flowers, one thing is certain, you are not the flower, you are the watcher. So watching is the key to meditation.

Watch your mind. Don't do anything – no repetition of a mantra, no repetition of the name of God. Just watch whatever the mind is doing. Don't disturb it, don't prevent it, don't repress it; don't do anything at all on your part. You just be a watcher. And the miracle of watching is meditation. As you watch, slowly, slowly, mind becomes empty of thoughts. But you are not falling asleep, you are becoming more alert, more aware. As the mind becomes completely empty, your whole energy becomes a flame of awakening. This flame is the result of meditation.

So you can say meditation is another name for watching, witnessing, observing – without any judgment, without any evaluation. Just by watching, you immediately get out of the mind; the watcher is never part of the mind. And as the watcher becomes more and more rooted and strong, the distance between the watcher and the mind goes on becoming longer and longer. Soon the mind is so far away that you can hardly feel that it exists – just an echo in faraway valleys. And ultimately, even those echoes disappear.

This disappearance of the mind is without your effort, without your using any force against the mind – just letting it die its own death. Once mind is absolutely silent, absolutely gone – you cannot find it anywhere – you become aware of yourself for the first time, because the same energy that was involved in the mind, finding no mind, turns upon itself.

Remember, energy is a constant movement. We say things are objects, and perhaps you have never thought why we call things objects. They are objects because they hinder your energy, your consciousness – they *object,* they are obstacles. But when there is no object, all thoughts, emotions, moods, everything has disappeared, you are in utter silence, in nothingness – rather, in no-thingness – the whole energy starts turning upon itself. This energy returning to the source brings immense delight.

When meditation comes back to its own source, it explodes in immense delight. This delight in its ultimate state is enlightenment. And anything that helps you to go through this process of meditation is discipline – perhaps taking a good bath, being clean and cool, sitting in a relaxed posture with eyes closed – neither hungry nor overloaded – sitting in the posture that is most relaxing, having a look at the whole body, every part, to see whether there is any tension. If there is any tension, then change the posture and bring the body into a relaxed state.

In the East it has been found, and found rightly, that the lotus posture – the way you must have seen the statues of Buddha sitting, that is called the lotus posture – it has been a discovery of thousands of years that it is the most relaxed state of the body. But for Westerners who are not accustomed to sit on the ground, the lotus posture is a nightmare; so avoid it, because it takes almost six months to learn the lotus posture – it is not necessary. If you are accustomed to sit on a chair, you can find a way, a posture, a chair made in a certain way, that helps your body to relax all its tensions. It does not matter whether you are sitting in a chair or in the lotus posture or lying down on a bed. Sitting is preferable because it will prevent you from falling asleep.

The lotus posture was chosen for many reasons. If one can manage it without torturing oneself, then it is the best, but it is not a necessity. It is certainly the best situation in which you can enter into watchfulness. The legs are crossed, the hands are crossed, the spine is straight; it gives many significant supports to being watchful.

First, in this position gravity has the least effect on the body, because your spine is straight, so gravity can affect only a very small portion. When you are lying down, gravity affects your whole body. That's why for sleep lying down is the best posture; gravity pulls the whole body, and because of its pull, the body loses all tensions.

Secondly, when you are lying down, if the purpose is to sleep then you should use a pillow, because the less blood reaches your mind, the less the mind will be active. The less blood reaches the mind, the more the possibility of falling asleep.

The lotus posture is a great combination – it has the least effect of gravity, and because the spine is straight, the least amount of blood reaches the mind, so mind cannot function: and in that posture, you cannot fall asleep easily. If you have learned the posture from your very birth, it becomes natural. The crossing of the legs, crossing of the hands, has a significance. Your body energy moves into a circle; the circle is not broken anywhere in a lotus posture. Both of your hands...this hand gives energy to the other hand, your one foot gives energy to the other foot, and the energy goes on moving in a circle. You become a circle of your bio-energy.

So, many things are of much help – your energy is not being released so you don't get tired; the least amount of blood is reaching your head so your mind does not function too much. You are sitting in such a position – your legs are locked, your hands are locked and your spine is straight – that sleep is difficult. These are just supports; they are not essential. It is not that one who cannot sit in a lotus posture cannot meditate; meditation will be a little difficult, but the lotus posture is only *helpful*, not absolutely needed.

It is better to follow the body and its wisdom. Use a chair; the whole thing is, you should be comfortable, so that the body does not draw your attention. That's why tension has to be avoided, because if you have a headache, then it will be difficult to meditate. Again and again your attention will go to the headache. If your leg is hurting, or if there is any slight tension anywhere in the body, it immediately alarms you. It is natural, and it is part of the body's wisdom; if it does not alarm, then there is danger. A snake may be biting you, and you may go on sitting. Your clothes may catch fire, your body may be burning, and you may not be aware of it. So the body immediately alarms wherever there is any trouble. That's the reason to create a relaxed position in which the body need not alarm you, because every alarm will be a disturbance in your meditation.

So the first discipline is a relaxed body; closed eyes, because if you have open eyes so many things are moving around, they can be a disturbance. It is perfectly right for beginners to use a blindfold so that you are completely inside, because it is your eyes, your senses, that take you outside. Eyes make eighty percent of all your outgoing contact – eighty percent is through the eyes. So close the eyes. For beginners, it is good if they can use ear-plugs – you close the ears so no noise from the outside disturbs you. It is only for beginners; all the precautions are for the beginners. And then just watch your mind – as if the mind is nothing but a traffic of thoughts, or a film, a movie passing on the TV screen. You are just a neutral observer. This is the discipline; and if this discipline is complete, watching comes very easily – and watching is meditation.

Through watchfulness, mind disappears, thoughts disappear; and that moment is the most blessed moment, when you are fully awake and there is not a single thought, just a silent sky of your inner being. This is the moment when energy turns inwards. The turning-in is sudden, abrupt; and as the energy turns inwards, it brings immense delight, orgasmic delight. And suddenly your awareness becomes so rich, because the energy is nourishment to your awareness. The energy coming back creates almost a flame of your being – you see all around pure light, silence, utter silence, and an immense centering. You are now at the very center.

At the very moment when you are exactly centered...the explosion. That explosion we call enlightenment. This enlightenment brings you all the treasures of the inner world, the whole splendor. It is the only miracle in the world to know oneself and to be oneself, and to know that one is deathless – one is beyond the body, beyond the mind, one is just pure consciousness.

So the discipline is just a support; the essential thing is witnessing, watching – that is meditation.

The Invitation, Session 21, August 31, 1987

# Ups and Downs

## Osho,

*In the last weeks I have seen a lot of old ghosts turning up again: impatience, competitiveness, perfectionism, lots of anger, and seriousness. What went wrong?*

The evolution of consciousness goes through many ups and downs. It is a hilly track. Many times it goes down just to go higher than before. It passes through valleys to reach to the peaks, and each peak is just the beginning of a new pilgrimage because a higher peak is ahead of you. But to reach the higher peak, you will have to go down again.

So the first thing to be remembered is: never be worried when days of down-going come; always keep your eyes on the faraway star. Those valleys are part of the mountains; you cannot take the valleys away and leave the mountains alone. Once this sinks deep into you, you will pass through the valleys dancing and singing, knowing perfectly well that a higher peak is waiting for you. And there is no end to this pilgrimage. Just as every day is followed by night, every height is followed by a down-going.

One has to learn not only to rejoice in the day but to rejoice in the night too – it has its own beauty. The peaks have their glory, the valleys have their richness. But if you become addicted to the peaks only, you have started choosing, and any consciousness that starts choosing gets into trouble. Remain choiceless, and whatever comes, enjoy it as part of natural growth.

The night may become even darker, but the darker the night becomes, the closer is the dawn. So rejoice in the darkening night, and learn to see the beauty of darkness, of the stars, because in the day you will not find those stars. And never compare what has been, and what should be, and what is.

What is has to be rejoiced in.

A life which knows no sadness, no tears, remains poor. Life has to know all the varieties of experiences to be rich. The more you know different aspects of existence, and still keep yourself together and centered, the more your life will find itself becoming richer and richer every moment, every day.

Always look at life as a dialectical process:

Here, night brings day.

Here, death brings new life.

Here, sadness brings a new rejoicing.

Here, emptiness brings a new fulfillment.

Everything is connected together…it is part of one organic whole. We create problems by dividing things. Learn the art – not to divide – but simply to remain alert, watchful, enjoying whatsoever life provides.

Just remember one thing: accept everything that life gives you. If it gives you darkness, enjoy it – dance under the stars on the dark night, remembering that every night is nothing but a womb for a new dawn, and every day is going to rest again in the darkness of the night.

When it is fall and the trees become naked and all the foliage falls down, just watch the old leaves flying in the wind in the forest, almost dancing. And the naked trees have a beauty of their own against the sky, but they are not going to remain naked forever. The old leaves have fallen just to give way to new leaves, new flowers.

Existence goes on renewing itself every moment. You should keep in tune with existence; never ask otherwise. That is the root cause of misery: when night is night, you cry for the day; when it is day, you cry for the repose of the night. Then life becomes a misery, a hell. You can make it a paradise by just accepting whatever is given to you with a grateful heart. Don't judge whether it is good or bad. Your gratefulness will transform everything into a beautiful experience, and will deepen your awareness, will heighten your love, will make you a beautiful flower with great fragrance.

Just learn the art of grateful acceptance. Gautam Buddha calls this the philosophy of *thusness:* whatever is, accept it as the nature of reality. Don't ever imagine to go against it. Never go against the current; just follow the river wherever it leads.

Two tramps sat with their backs against a tree. "You know, Jim," the first tramp mused, "this business of tramping your way through life is not what it is cracked up to be; wandering, unwanted everywhere, sneered at by your fellow men."

"Well," observed the second tramp, "if that's the way you feel about it, why don't you go and find yourself a job?"

"What?" exclaimed his friend, "And admit that I'm a failure!"

Never admit that you're a failure. The secret of total acceptance is the secret of absolute success; you cannot fail. There is no power anywhere that can make you a failure, because even in failure you will be dancing and rejoicing. Transform every opportunity into something creative and beautiful.

I don't want you to get the illusory idea of remaining permanently in the same state of mind; that is possible only if you are dead. If you are alive, climates will change, seasons will change; and you have to learn through winters, through summers, through rains. You have to pass through all these seasons with a dance in your heart, knowing perfectly well that existence is never against you, so whatever it gives...it may be bitter, but it is medicine. It may not taste sweet to you in the beginning, but finally you will find it has given you something which just one state of mind could not have given.

So whatever is happening is good. Take it easy. This will not stay, this will also change.

But don't make any effort to change it.

Leave it up to existence.

This is what I call trust.

Existence is wiser than you and will provide you all the opportunities needed for your growth.

The New Dawn, Session 2, June 19, 1987

# A Friendly Relationship

## Osho,

*How can one be meditating every day, and have a mind which becomes more and more noisy?*

The question you have asked has many implications. First, one has to understand that your mind is very ancient. It is the history of the whole universe from the very beginning.

It has been working so long, so efficiently, that scientists say they have not yet been able to create a computer which can compete with the human mind. And the human mind is placed in a small space in your skull; *their* computers are placed in big rooms. One scientist has calculated that it would need almost one square mile of space for a computer comparable to the human mind. The human mind is a miracle, one of the greatest miracles in biology, in the evolution of man. Mind is simply unbelievable.

You don't know anything about it, the way it works, although it is *your* mind. You don't know how it accumulates millions of memories. The scientists have calculated that a single man's mind can contain all the libraries of the world. He can memorize everything that has ever been written, down the ages. That is the capacity; you may use it, you may not use it. And the very idea that a single human mind has the capacity to memorize all that is written in all the books that are in existence in the whole world...it simply baffles. It looks unbelievable.

You don't know what your mind is doing for you. Your mind is regulating everything in your body; otherwise, how do you think that for seventy or eighty years, or even a hundred years... And there are people who have passed that; they have reached their one hundred and fiftieth birthday, and there are a few hundred people in the Soviet Union who have passed the age of one hundred and eighty... Scientists say there is no reason for the body to die for at least three hundred years. It is just an old hypnosis, autohypnosis, which has made the idea prevalent that you have only seventy years to live. It goes so deep in your consciousness that by the seventieth year you start thinking you are sinking, you are gone. Anyway by the time you are retired at the age of sixty there is nothing to do. Death seems to be a relief, not a danger.

We have not been capable enough and human enough to provide some dignity, some self-respect, some pride for our old people. We have not been able to find dimensions where they can contribute to the world. They are experienced and certainly capable enough – enough for their self-respect, enough for them to live and not to feel like a burden.

When George Bernard Shaw became seventy years old, he started taking trips to small villages around London. His friends were surprised: "What are you doing? For days you disappear. In this old age you should rest."

He said, "I'm searching for a place to rest, in this old age."

They said, "What do you mean? You have a beautiful house, you have everything that you need."

He said, "You don't understand. I'm going around all these villages looking into the cemeteries, at the gravestones, in search of a place where people have lived at least a hundred years."

And finally he found a village where on a gravestone was the inscription, "This man died at the untimely age of a hundred and twenty." He said, "This is the village worth living in, where people think that at the age of one hundred and twenty it is an untimely death." He lived in that village and he lived for more than a hundred years. Perhaps it has some significance, not just accidental. He was a man of tremendous wisdom. And if the villagers believe, then the atmosphere is bound to change his own conditioning.

Scientists say that man's body has the capacity, this is the minimum, to live at least three hundred years. But why does man not live so long? Perhaps man does not know how to live; perhaps man does not know how to use his body, how to use his mind.

Mind is a great miracle. Existence has not been able to create anything higher than your mind. Its function is so complex that it baffles the greatest scientists. It manages your whole body, and it has such a complex system. Who manages that a certain part of your blood should go to the brain? Who manages that only a certain amount of oxygen should reach the brain? Who manages what part of your food should become bones, should become blood, should become skin? Who manages that part of your skin should become nails, and part of your skin should become eyes, one part of your skin should become ears? Certainly *you* are not managing it, and I don't see any other manager around.

So first you have to be grateful to the mind. That is the first step to go beyond mind; not as an enemy but as a friend. I have a tremendous respect for the mind. We are so much obliged to the mind, there is no way to return our gratitude.

So the first thing is: Meditation is not *against* mind, it is *beyond* mind. And beyond is not equivalent to against; that misunderstanding spreads the more people talk about meditation, particularly people who don't understand meditation – those who have read about it, those who know the techniques. Techniques are simple; they are available in many scriptures, you can read them...

A master will never become irrelevant for the simple reason...because who will teach you to love the mind and yet go beyond it, to love your body, to respect your body, to have gratitude towards your mind? It is a tremendous, miraculous functioning. That will make a friendship between you and the mind. With this friendship deepening, whenever you are meditating, the mind will not disturb because your meditation is not against it. It is in fact its own fulfillment, it is its own flowering. Going beyond it is not an antagonistic attitude but a friendly evolution.

So this should be the background of all meditators: not to be a fighter. If you fight, you may be able to make the mind quiet for some time, but it is not your victory. The mind will come back – you will need it. You cannot live without it, you cannot exist in the world without it. And if you can create a friendly relationship with the mind, a loving bridge, rather than a hindrance to meditation it starts becoming a help. It protects your silence, because that silence is also *its* own treasure, it is not just yours. It becomes a soil in which the roses of meditation will blossom, and the soil will be as happy as the roses. When the roses are dancing in the sun, in the rain, in the wind, the soil will also rejoice.

To me, meditation is the very soul of religion. But it can be attained only if you move rightly; just a single step in a wrong direction... And you are always moving on a razor's edge.

Begin with love of the body, which is your outermost part. Start loving your mind – and if you love your mind you will decorate it, just the way you decorate your body. You keep it clean, you keep it fresh; you don't want your body to smell horrible to people. You want your body to be loved and respected by others. Your presence should not be simply tolerated, but welcomed.

You have to decorate your mind with poetry, with music, with art, with great literature. Your trouble is, your mind is filled only with trivia. Such third-rate things go on through your mind that you cannot love it; you think of nothing which is great. Make it more in tune with the greatest poets. Make it more in tune with people like Fyodor Dostoyevski, Leo Tolstoy, Anton Chekov, Turgenev, Rabindranath Tagore, Kahlil Gibran, Mikhail Naimy. Make it filled with the greatest heights that mind has reached. Then you will not be unfriendly to the mind. Then you will rejoice in the mind. Even if the mind is there in your silence, it will have a poetry and a music of its own. And to transcend such a refined mind is easy. It is a friendly step towards higher peaks; poetry turning into mysticism, great literature turning into great insights about existence, music turning into silence.

And as these things start turning into higher peaks, beyond mind, you will be discovering new worlds, new universes for which we don't even have a name. We can say blissfulness, ecstasy, enlightenment, but no word fully describes it. It is simply outside the power of language to reduce it to explanations, to theories, to philosophies. It is simply beyond...but mind rejoices in its transcendence.

I don't think that anybody who is against his body and against his mind is capable of reaching the beyond.

Only love is the path.

Make your mind as beautiful as possible. Decorate it with flowers. First let your mind be decorated. Only through this perfumed garden of the mind will you be able silently to go beyond without any fight. Mind will be a help, not a hindrance.

I have not found it to be a hindrance; hence I can say with absolute authority it is not a hindrance. You just don't know how to use it.

The Great Pilgrimage, Session 13, September 12, 1987

# The Eternal Life Within You

## Osho,

*Can you talk about acceptance of death?*

Human languages are very poor. The word "acceptance" has a hidden reluctance in it. You may not have looked into the word, but when you say, "accept it," there is a hidden reluctance, a kind of compulsoriness because there is nothing else to do. So why make a fuss about it? – accept it.

This kind of acceptance is not true and authentic. I would say, enjoy it. Unless your acceptance is enjoyment, unless your acceptance is wholehearted, without any reluctance, not out of any compulsion, not out of a particular situation but out of your understanding... Acceptance becomes a beautiful experience if it is at the same time enjoyment. You are not accepting under the pressure of circumstances; you are accepting on your own accord, with joy, with a deep welcome. Then only you understand what acceptance can do to your being. In a single moment it can change you, transform you from an ordinary human being into an awakened human being.

But don't accept reluctantly. That is deceiving yourself, as if deep down you don't want to accept. Authentic acceptance has no negative tone in it, no reluctance, no resistance, no compulsion. It is not because of the pressure of things and situations and our helplessness. Don't accept out of helplessness, accept out of your strength.

Authentic living needs great intensity and great totality, not a thin layer. A lukewarm survival is not living. But if you know that the next moment you are going to die, you will drop everything that you were involved in, and the only priority will be to know yourself.

Before death comes at least be aware who you are.

You don't have time to postpone.

It happened that one man used to come to a mystic, Eknath, for many years. He was a devotee but there was a doubt in his mind that was continuously pinching him. And because there were always many disciples he could not ask. So one day he came very early, before sunrise. Eknath was just coming out of the river. He had taken a bath before his morning meditation in the temple. The man reached Eknath and said, "Forgive me for disturbing you at this time, but I have been carrying a question my whole life" – he was a young man, healthy, strong. He said, "And I cannot dissolve it, it continues. It is a disturbance between me and you."

Eknath said, "What is the problem?"

He said, "The problem is that I have seen you for many years, but I have never seen you sad, I have never seen you angry, I have never seen you jealous; I have never seen you in any negative state of mind. You are always smiling and always joyous and relaxed, as if there is no worry in the world, no problem in the world. You don't seem to be concerned even about death. You take it so lightly.

"And the problem is that a doubt arises in me whether you are an actor or you are really enlightened – because one can make oneself act a smile, always showing joyousness, taking everything lightly, never seriously. Is it just a discipline? Have you trained yourself for it, or is it something that has happened to you? Is it not your doing but a natural, spontaneous understanding that has arisen out of your meditations? That question has been bothering me, because a man can manage to pretend. You see actors in films and you know they are the most miserable lot in the world, but in the film they look so joyous, so happy, so loving, so peaceful, so courageous. If this is possible in a film or in a drama, then why is it not possible in real life? You just need a little control not to show your real feelings but always to go on acting."

Eknath said, "Wait a minute. Before I answer your question I should not forget something that I wanted to tell you. I have been forgetting for three days, and it is important. So first I will tell you that thing and then I will answer your question. Just three or four days ago I happened to look at your hand, and I was very much shocked. Your lifeline is finished; just such a small fraction remains that you may be able to live seven days at the most. On the seventh day as the sun is setting you will be dying. This I have been forgetting and this is more important than your question. Now we can discuss your question."

The man stood up. He said, "I don't have any question and I don't have any time to discuss! If death is coming within seven days, why should I worry whether you are real or unreal? That is *your* business – it is not my problem."

The man started going down the steps. There were many steps to the temple, and Eknath watched him: just five minutes ago he had come so strong, so young, and now he was going just like an old man, wobbling, taking the support of the railing that he had never taken before, afraid to fall. And when he reached home he simply went to bed directly, even though it was not the time; it was morning, he had just got up from the bed. He collected the whole family and told them what Eknath had said. It was inconceivable that Eknath would lie; there was no point in his lying. So there was crying and weeping, and the man stopped eating – what is the point now when you are not going to live?

But a strange thing started happening as he became settled with the idea that death is coming, and nothing can be done: "Why not use this time for the meditation that I have been postponing for many years? Eknath goes on saying every day to meditate, put your energy into discovering yourself, and I have been postponing it, because what is the hurry? I am a young man and these things – meditation and knowing yourself – belong to the old people when they have nothing else to do. Anyway they are out of work, retired. That is the right time to meditate and find out who you are. Right now you have to find many other things – money, power, prestige, respectability. This is not the time to waste in finding yourself. That you can do at any moment when you will not be of any use in life, and life will reject you by retiring you."

It is strange that everywhere when people are retired, their colleagues gather together just to say goodbye to them, and they always give them a pocket watch. That I could not believe. What is the idea? But now I know. They give them a pocket watch as, "Not much time is left to remind you, but now, do the essential things that you have been postponing."

The man lay down, started watching his mind for the first time, and became utterly silent within two, three days. But the whole family and other relatives and friends from far away arrived. They were even more disturbed. Death is coming; that is a shock. And what has happened to this man? He does not open his eyes, he does not eat, he does not take any interest. This was a time to meet the family, the friends, because who knows when you will ever meet these people again? There is not much chance. But he is not interested in anything.

He did not even allow them to call a physician. By the fourth day they could not believe that he was looking so beautiful, so graceful, so silent. His whole bedroom had almost the same quality which exists around a man of silence or which exists in a living temple, where not only statues are but some living master is also present.

People came with great words, prepared dialogues which one needs to say, because it is very embarrassing to come to a man who is going to die. What to say to him? You cannot talk about movies, you cannot talk about politics, you cannot talk about football games, you cannot talk about boxing. What is there to talk about? It is very embarrassing if somebody is dying and you have to leave. Then one prepares a dialogue to console him: "Don't be worried; everybody dies. It is not that it is happening only to you. And then there is God: You have been a virtuous man, and your heaven is absolutely guaranteed." One has to prepare things like that because now, the worldly things that one gossips about with each other are of no point.

But as they entered, even this dialogue was not possible, the man was so silent. On the seventh day he opened his eyes and asked his family, "How much time is left for the sun to set?"

Reading this story I remember why that pocket watch is given to people: so they don't even need to ask anybody else; just look at your pocket watch and be finished! Never present a pocket watch to anybody, because that simply means that you have taken it for granted that this man is gone. The pocket watch is the last present.

And the people said, "The sun is just about to set within a few minutes." He was showing such grace, such joy, such blissfulness, that the family could not believe what a metamorphosis these seven days have been. They all knew he was an ordinary man. The wife knew, the father knew, the brothers knew that he had nothing special, but in seven days he has gone far beyond them.

Exactly as the sun was setting they all started crying and weeping. And he was saying to them, "Be quiet. There is nothing to worry about."

At that moment Eknath arrived. The whole family touched his feet and told him, "Save him! Can you do anything?"

Eknath said, "With death there is no possibility. Just let me see him."

So they all respectfully moved and gave way to Eknath. The man was sitting silently with closed eyes, looking almost like a marble statue of Gautam Buddha...in just seven days, and he was an ordinary person. Eknath called his name and said, "I have come to see you and to tell you that it was only a device. You are not going to die. You have a lifeline that is very long. You will live almost as much as you have lived. You have lived only half the lifeline, so there are many years to live. This was a way to answer you, your question."

The man said, "My God! I had never thought that this was a way to answer my question."

Eknath said, "There was no other way. Whatever I would have said to you, you would have remained with doubts. A man who can pretend for years to be happy can also lie that he is enlightened. I wanted to give you some experience of it, that it is not acting. And these seven days have given you the experience. Have you received the answer or not?"

The man stood up, jumped out of bed – for seven days he had not left the bed at all – touched the feet of Eknath and said, "Your compassion is great. If your compassion had not been so great you would not have lied. But you have answered my question. Now there is no doubt at all. And I cannot see that any doubt is possible in the future. I have known the space in which you are living."

Eknath said, "It does not matter whether you are going to die after seven days or seventy years. Once you become aware that you are going to die, it does not matter when."

The awareness of death makes you live life as totally, as joyously, as possible. Death is not your enemy. In fact, it is an invitation for you to live intensely, totally, to squeeze every drop of juice from every moment. Death is a tremendous challenge and invitation. Without death there would not have been any Gautam

Buddha, any Jesus, any Lao Tzu, any Tilopa. There would not have been any Kabir, any Raidas, any Mansoor, any Sarmad.

It is death and its awareness that makes you live as totally, as deeply, as consciously as possible – because before death knocks on your doors you should be able to see the eternal life within you. Then there is no death; death is a fiction. It is a reality only to those who have not lived, not lived life in its completeness, in its entirety.

For those who have lived there is no death.

It is only a change – just changing the house.

The man who knows himself, knows death as only a change of house. "Acceptance" is not the right word, but there is no other word; this is the difficulty. I would say, rejoice; make every day a celebration. And if you can make all these days a celebration, your death will be found to be a fiction. These days of celebration and meditation and silence and joy and love will create in you the capacity to die consciously. And one who dies consciously knows that death is nothing but changing his house. And it is always for a better house because life always goes upwards; it is an evolutionary process.

God created everything so there is no question of any evolution. He created monkeys as monkeys, and he created men and men – not that the monkeys have evolved into man; there is no evolution. God has made the world perfect. Evolution is possible only if things are imperfect.

Evolution should take on a different dimension, an inner evolution.

I want man to evolve.

Man can evolve into a new man. But that evolution will happen only through deep meditation, watchfulness, waiting and accepting life with joy, and accepting death with joy, with no reluctance, without any pressure, but from your innermost feeling.

Everything that is, is beautiful.

It can be more beautiful – there is no limit to evolution. Particularly for consciousness there is no limit; it can go even beyond Gautam Buddha, beyond Bodhidharma, beyond all the great, awakened people of the past, because consciousness has no limits. It is as vast as the sky, as the whole universe.

Just a little joke... A good laugh is the greatest prayer.

A little boy on a picnic strays away from his family and

suddenly realizes he is lost and night is falling. After running around and shouting for a while, he becomes very frightened and kneels down to pray with uplifted hands. "Dear Lord," he says, "please help me to find my mummy and daddy and I promise I won't hit my sister anymore."

Just then a bird flies overhead and shits right into his outstretched hands. The boy examines it, looks up to heaven and says, "Lord, don't give me this shit, I really am lost."

Everybody is really lost. Very few people have reached their home. But your pilgrimage of finding your home should not be serious and sad and heavy; it should be of laughter and song and dance. If you can find your home dancing, laughing, it is true finding. By sadness and seriousness you are bound to find some graveyard, not your home.

We need people who are seekers, but not serious. That kind of seeking – serious and sad – has not led man anywhere.

The Invitation, Session 18, August 30, 1987

# Make Love Your Very Quality

*T*HE MIRACLE IS, if you meditate and slowly slowly get out of the ego and out of your personality and realize your real self, love will come on its own. You don't have to do anything; it is a spontaneous flowering. But it blossoms only in a certain climate, and that climate I call meditation. In the climate of silence, no-mind, no disturbance inside, absolute clarity, peace and silence, suddenly you will see thousands of flowers have opened within you. And their fragrance is love.

Naturally, first you will love yourself, because that will be your first encounter. First you will become aware of the fragrance that is arising in you and the light that was born in you, and the blissfulness that is showering on you. Then loving will become your nature. Then you will love many; then you will love all.

In fact, what we know in our ignorance is a relationship, and what we know in our awareness is no longer a relationship. It is not that I love you, it is that I *am* love.

You have to understand the difference. When you say, "I love you," what about others? What about the whole existence? The narrower your love is, the more imprisoned. Its wings are cut; it cannot fly in the sky across the sun. It does not have freedom; it is almost in a golden cage. The cage is beautiful, but inside the cage the bird is not the same bird that you see in the sky, opening its wings.

Love has not to become a relationship, not a narrowing but a broadening. Love has to become your very quality, your very character, your very being, your radiance. Just as the sun radiates light not for anyone in particular, unaddressed, meditation radiates love unaddressed. Of course, first it is felt within oneself, for oneself, and then it starts radiating all around. Then you love not only human beings, you love trees, you love birds; you simply love, you *are* love.

Just don't listen to the priests. They are the enemies of love. They have been teaching the world to hate yourself and to hate the world, because they have been teaching either it is a sin that you are born or it is because of your evil acts in a past life that you are suffering in this life. But no religion accepts this life with joy and rejoicing, as a gift, as a reward of which you are not worthy, to which you don't claim any right – you have not earned it.

So the first thing is: avoid the priests. They have taught you life-negative values. And my effort here is to bring back life-affirmation. That's what I call loving yourself: accepting yourself not as a sinner. How can you accept yourself if you think you are a sinner? How can you love yourself if you think you are nothing but full of guilt, nothing but an accumulated past of evil acts of millions of lives? You will hate yourself.

And that's what your priests have been trying: renounce life, hate life, hate pleasure, hate everything, and sacrifice everything if you want to enter into paradise. Nobody has ever returned from paradise, so there is no evidence of any paradise anywhere, no proof. It is just a futile exercise which has never been able to come to a conclusion.

The old priest was warning his congregation about sin. "Sin," he said, "is like a big dog. There is the big dog of pride, and the big dog of envy, and the big dog of greed, and finally, there is the big dog of sex. And you have to kill those big dogs before they prevent you from getting to heaven. It can be done, I know, because over the years I have done it. I killed the big dog of envy, the big dog of pride, the big dog of greed – and yes, my children, I killed the big dog of sex."

"Father," came a voice from the back of the church, "are you sure that the last dog did not die a natural death?"

You cannot change nature. If you can simply live naturally, transformations come. If they come, then sex disappears, but not by your efforts.

By your efforts it goes on hanging around you. The more you

repress it, the more you have it. The more you live it, the more is the possibility to go beyond it.

An old couple were sitting at home one evening listening to the faith healer on the radio.

"Okay, folks," he began, "God wants to heal you all. All you have to do is put one hand on the radio and the other hand on the part that is sick."

The old lady got up, shuffled over to the radio and put her hand on her arthritic hip. Then the old man put one hand on the radio and the other hand on his fly. His wife looked at him in contempt and said, "You old idiot. The man said he would heal the sick – not raise the dead!"

Live naturally. Live peacefully. Live inwardly. Just give a little time to yourself, being alone, being silent, just watching the inner scene of your mind. Slowly, slowly thoughts disappear. Slowly, slowly, one day the mind is so still, so silent, as if it is not there. Just this silence...in this moment you are not here.

In this silence within you, you will find a new dimension of life. In this dimension greed does not exist, sex does not exist, anger does not exist, violence does not exist. It is not a credit to you; it is the new dimension beyond mind where love exists pure, unpolluted by any biological urge; where compassion exists for no other reason, not to get any reward in heaven, because compassion is a reward unto itself.

And a deep longing exists to share all that treasure that you have discovered within yourself, and to shout from the housetops to the people, "You are not poor – paradise is within you. You need not be beggars, you are born emperors – you have just to discover your empire." And your empire is not of the outside world, your empire is of your own interiority. It is within you and it has always been there, just waiting for you to come home. Love will come, and will come in abundance; so much that you cannot contain it, you will find that it is overflowing you, it is reaching in all directions.

Just discover your hidden splendor. Life can be simply a song – a song of joy. Life can be simply a dance, a celebration, a continuous celebration. All that you have to do is to learn a life-affirmative lifestyle.

I call religious only that man who is life-affirmative. All those who are life-negative may *think* they are religious, they are not. Their sadness shows they are not. Their seriousness shows they are not.

A man of authentic religion will have a sense of humor.

It is *our* universe, it is our home. We are not orphans. This earth is our mother, this sky is our father. This whole vast universe is for us and we are for it. In fact, there is no division between us and the whole. We are organically joined with it, we are part of one orchestra.

To feel this music of existence is the only religion that I can accept as authentic, as valid. It does not have any scriptures, it need not have. It does not have any statutes of god, because it does not believe in any hypothesis. It has nothing to worship, it has only to be silent, and out of that silence comes gratitude, prayer, and the whole existence turns to godliness.

There is no god as a person. God is spread all over: in the trees, in the birds, in the animals, in humanity, in the wise, in the other-wise… All that is alive is nothing but godliness, ready to open its wings, ready to fly into the freedom, ultimate freedom of consciousness.

Yes, you will love yourself and you will love the whole existence too.

The Invitation, Session 30, September 5, 1987

# Laughter Brings Strength

## Osho,

*You have brought laughter into the autumn of my days. I have heard that laughter is the best medicine. Can this be true?*

Medical science says that laughter is one of the most deep-going medicines that nature has provided man with. If you can laugh when you are ill, you will get your health back sooner. If you cannot laugh even if you are healthy, sooner or later you will lose your health and you will become ill. Laughter brings some energy from your inner source to the surface. Energy starts flowing, follows laughter like a shadow.

Have you watched it? When you really laugh, for those few moments you are in a deep meditative state. Thinking stops. It is impossible to laugh and think together. They are diametrically opposite: either you can laugh or you can think. If you really laugh, thinking stops. If you are still thinking, laughter will be just so-so, lagging behind. It will be a crippled laughter.

When you really laugh, suddenly mind disappears.

As far as I know, dancing and laughter are the best, natural, easily approachable doors. If you really dance, thinking stops. You go on and on, you whirl and whirl, and you become a whirlpool – all boundaries, all divisions, are lost. You don't even know where your body ends and where existence begins. You melt into existence and existence melts into you; there is an overlapping of boundaries. And if you are really dancing – not managing it but allowing it to manage you, allowing it to possess you – if you are possessed by dance, thinking stops.

The same happens with laughter. If you are possessed by laughter, thinking stops. And if you know a few moments of no-mind, those glimpses will promise you many more rewards that are going to come. You just have to become more and more of the sort, of the quality, of no-mind. More and more, thinking has to be dropped.

Laughter can be a beautiful introduction to a non-thinking state. And the beauty is...there are methods – for example, you can concentrate on a flame or on a black dot, or you can concentrate on a mantra, but the greater possibility is that by the time the mind is disappearing you will start feeling sleepy, you will fall asleep.

When thinking disappears, there are two alternatives left: either you move into *satori* – a fully alert, no-thought state – or a fully asleep, no-thought state. And sleep is more natural because you have practiced it so long. If you live sixty years, twenty years, you have been asleep. It is the greatest activity that you have been doing; one third of your life is spent in sleep. In no other exercise do you spend so much time and so much energy.

America is the only country which is suffering from sleeplessness so tremendously. Insomnia has become almost common. If after forty you have not started suffering from insomnia, that simply means you are a failure, that you could not succeed – in business, in politics. In power you couldn't succeed; you are a failure. All successful people suffer from insomnia, have to suffer. They suffer from ulcers, have to suffer. So remember: insomnia, ulcers and things like that are nothing but certificates of success – that you have succeeded.

Repeating a mantra – monotonous, the same again and again – the mind loses interest in it, starts falling asleep. That's the beauty of laughter: you cannot fall asleep. Laughing, how can you fall asleep? It brings a state of no-mind and no-thought, and does not allow you to fall asleep.

In a few Zen monasteries, every monk has to start his morning with laughter, and has to end his night with laughter – the first thing and the last thing! You try it. It is very beautiful. It will look a little crazy – mm? – because so many serious people are all around. They will not understand. If you are happy, they always ask why. The question is foolish! If you are sad, they never ask why. They take it for granted – if you are sad, it's okay. Everybody is sad. What is new in it? Even if you want to tell them, they are not interested because they know all about it, they are not interested because they know all about, they themselves are sad. So what is the point of telling a long story? – cut it short!

But if you are laughing for no reason, then they become alert – something has gone wrong. This man seems to be a little crazy because only crazy people enjoy laughter; only in madhouses will you find crazy people laughing. This is unfortunate, but this is so.

It will be difficult, if you are a husband or a wife it will be difficult to suddenly laugh early in the morning. Try it – it pays tremendously. It is one of the most beautiful moods to get up with, to get out of bed with. For *no* reason – because there *is* no reason. Simply, you are again there, still alive – it is a miracle! It seems ridiculous! Why are you alive? And again the world is there. Your wife is still snoring, and the same room, and the same house. In this constantly changing world – what Hindus call the *maya* – at least for one night nothing has changed. Everything is there: you can hear the milkman and the traffic has started, and the same noises – it is worth laughing at!

One day you will not get up in the morning. One day the milkman will knock at the door, the wife will be snoring, but you will not be there. One day, death will come. Before it knocks you down, have a good laugh – while there is time, have a good laugh.

And look at the whole ridiculousness: again the same day starts – you have done the same things again and again for your whole life. Again you will get into your slippers, rush to the bathroom – for what? Brushing your teeth, taking a shower – for what? Where are you going? Getting ready and nowhere to go! Dressing, rushing to the office – for what? Just to do the same thing tomorrow?

Look at the whole ridiculousness of it – and have a good laugh. Don't open your eyes. The moment you see that sleep is gone, first start laughing, then open your eyes – and that will set a trend for the whole day. If you can laugh early in the morning you will laugh the whole day. You have created a chain effect; one thing leads to another. Laughter leads to more laughter.

And almost always I have seen people doing just the wrong thing. From the very early morning they get out of bed complaining, gloomy, sad, depressed, miserable. Then one thing leads to another – and for *nothing*. And they get angry…it is very bad because it will change your climate for the whole day, it will set a pattern for the whole day.

Zen people are more sane. In their insanity they are saner than you. They start with laughter...and then the whole day you will feel laughter bubbling, welling up. There are so many ridiculous things happening all over! God must be dying of laughter – down the centuries, for eternity, seeing this ridiculousness of the world. The people that he has created, and all the absurdities – it is *really* a comedy. He must be laughing. If you become silent after your laughter, one day you will hear God also laughing, you will hear the whole existence laughing – trees and stones and stars with you.

And the Zen monk goes to sleep in the night again with laughter. The day is over, the drama is closed again – with laughter he says, "Goodbye, and if I survive again, tomorrow morning I will greet you again with laughter."

Try it! Start and finish your day with laughter, and you will see, by and by, in between these two, more and more laughter starts happening. And the more laughing you become, the more religious.

A Sudden Clash of Thunder, Session 9, August 19, 1976

# The Sheer Delight

YOU WERE NOT here and the world was here; you will not be here one day and the world is going to be here. How can you possess it? How can you claim that "I am the owner"? How can you say anything? And if you are meditative, your whole life will become a sharing. You will give whatsoever you can give – your love, your understanding, your compassion – whatsoever you can you will give, your energy, body, mind, soul, whatsoever. And you will enjoy it.

There is no greater enjoyment than that of sharing something. Have you given something to somebody? That's why people enjoy giving gifts so much. It is a sheer delight. When you give something to somebody – maybe valueless, may not be of much value, but just the way, just the gesture that you give, satisfies tremendously. Just think of a person whose life is a gift! Whose every moment is sharing – he lives in heaven. There is no other heaven than that.

A Sudden Clash of Thunder, "Laugh Your Way to God,"
Session 9, August 19, 1976

# Reach
# for the Stars

JUST AS MISERY can be contagious, health can also be.

One lighted being is bound to create an urgent, instant longing in others to have the same light. One person dancing and singing with abandon is bound to affect people because they are also carrying the same song hidden, the same dance – they have been crippled by their society. They also have the same eyes for beauty but they have been blinded by the society. They have also the energy to celebrate, but this society does not believe in celebration.

This society is absolutely insane. It believes in money, it believes in power, it believes in violence, it believes in rapes, it believes in murder. It believes in all kinds of crimes, and it believes in all kinds of fictions, but it does not understand even a little bit about itself.

The moment a small window opens into you, you are a transformed being. The new man is born in you.

Enjoy – this existence is for your enjoyment, it is our existence, it is our home. Nobody is a sinner except those who don't celebrate. To me, celebration is the only virtue.

A man was visiting his friend, George, who was in the hospital dying.

The friend said, "Well, anyway, George, you have lived a good life. For sure you will be going to heaven."

George replied, "Yes, I have lived a good life, but there is something I never told you."

"What is that?" asked his friend.

"Remember that time I went to Chicago on business last year? Well, I made love with a beautiful woman there."

Shocked, his friend replied, "I can't believe it. I mean, your wife, your kids – did you not think about them?"

"Yes, I did," replied George, "and then I thought, since I already knew what hell was like I might as well see what heaven is like."

You have known hell, now you are entering into heaven. Everybody has suffered for many lives in hell. Hell is nowhere in the geography of the world, of the universe; it is in your distorted mind, another name of a distorted mind. And heaven is another name of a mind which has transcended itself and reached into a space of no-mind. Hence my insistence continuously on silence.

Blessed are those who allow themselves to be contagious with festivity, to love, to peace, to silence, to celebration.

The Great Pilgrimage, Session 12, September 11, 1987

# Maturity: the Seed that has Blossomed

## Osho,

*What are the qualities of a mature person?*

The qualities of a mature person are very strange.

First, he is not a person. He is no longer a self. He has a presence, but he is not a person.

Second, he is more like a child – simple and innocent.

That's why I said the qualities of a mature person are very strange, because "maturity" gives the sense as if he has experienced, he is aged, old. Physically he may be old but spiritually he is an innocent child. His maturity is not just experience gained through life. Then he will not be a child, and then he will not be a presence; he will be an experienced person – knowledgeable but not mature.

Maturity has nothing to do with your life experiences. It has something to do with your inward journey, experiences of the inner.

The more he goes deeper into himself, the more mature he is. When he has reached the very center of his being he is perfectly mature. But at that moment the person disappears, only presence remains; the self disappears, only silence remains; the knowledge disappears, only innocence remains.

To me, maturity is another name for realization. You have come to the fulfillment of your potential. It has become actual. The seed has come on the long journey and has blossomed.

Maturity has a fragrance. It gives a tremendous beauty to the individual. It gives intelligence, the sharpest possible intelligence. It makes him nothing but love. His action is love, his inaction is love; his life is love, his death is love. He is just a flower of love.

The West has definitions of maturity which are very childish. The West means by maturity that you are no longer innocent, that you have ripened through life experiences, that you cannot be cheated easily, that you cannot be exploited; that you have within you something like a solid rock – a protection, a security. This definition is very ordinary, very worldly. Yes, in the world you will find mature people of this type. But the way I see maturity is totally different, diametrically opposite to this definition. Maturity will not make you a rock; it will make you so vulnerable, so soft, so simple.

I remember...a thief entered a master's hut. It was a fullmoon night, and he had entered by mistake; otherwise, what can you find in a master's house? The thief was looking, and was amazed that there was nothing. And then suddenly he saw the man, who was coming with a candle in his hand.

And the master said, "What are you looking for in the dark? Why did you not wake me up? I was just sleeping near the front door, and I could have showed you the whole house!" The man looked so simple and so innocent, as if he could not conceive that anybody could be a thief.

Before his simplicity and innocence, the thief said, "Perhaps you do not know that I am a thief."

The master said, "That doesn't matter – one has to be *something*. The real thing is that I have been in the house for thirty years and I have not found anything, so let us search together! And if we can find something, we can be partners. I have not found anything in this house – it is just empty."

The thief was a little afraid – the man seems to be strange. Either he is mad or...who knows what kind of man he is? He wanted to escape, because he had brought things from two other houses that he had left outside the house.

The master had only one blanket – that was all that he had – and it was a cold night, so he told that thief, "Don't go in this way, don't insult me this way; otherwise I will never be able to forgive myself, that a poor man came to my house in the middle of the night and had to go empty-handed. Just take this blanket. And it will be good – outside it is so cold. I am inside the house; it is warmer here."

He covered the thief with his blanket. The thief was just losing his mind! He said, "What are you doing? I am a *thief!*"

The master said, "That does not matter. In this world everybody has to be somebody, has to do something. You may be stealing; that doesn't matter, a profession is a profession. Just do it well, with all my blessings. Do it perfectly. Don't be caught; otherwise you will be in trouble."

The thief said, "You are strange. You are naked and you don't have anything."

The master said, "Don't be worried, because I am coming with you! Only the blanket was keeping me in this house – otherwise in this house there is nothing – and the blanket I have given to you. I am coming with you; we will live together. And you seem to have many things – it is a good partnership. I have given my all to you. You can give me a little bit, and that will be right."

The thief could not believe it. He just wanted to escape from that place and from that man. He said, "No, I cannot take you with me. I have my wife, I have my children... And my neighbors, what will they say? – 'You have brought a naked man!' "

He said, "That's right. I will not put you in any embarrassing situation. So you can go, I will remain in this house." And as the thief was going, the master shouted, "Hey! Come back!" The thief had never heard such a strong voice, which went just like a knife, and he had to come back.

The master said, "Learn some ways of courtesy. I have given you the blanket and you have not even thanked me. So first, thank me – it will help you a long way. Secondly, going out – you opened the door when you came in – close the door! Can't you see the night is so cold, and can't you see that I have given you the blanket and I am naked? Your being a thief is okay, but as far as manners are concerned, I am a difficult man. I cannot tolerate this kind of behavior. Say thank you!"

And the thief had to say, "Thank you, sir." He closed the door and escaped. He could not believe what had happened, could not sleep the whole night. Again and again he remembered...he had never heard such a strong voice. Such power – and the man had nothing! Then he inquired the next day and he found out that he was a great master.

The thief had not done good – it was absolutely ugly to go to that poor man; he had nothing. But he was a great master. The thief said, "I can understand, myself, that he is a very strange kind of man. In my whole life I have been coming in contact with different kinds of people, from the poorest to the richest, but never... Even remembering him, a shivering goes through my body. "When he called me back I could not run away. I was absolutely free, I could have taken the things and run away, but I could not. There was something in his voice that pulled me back."

After a few months he was caught, and in the court the magistrate asked him, "Can you name a person who knows you in this vicinity?"

He said, "Yes, one person knows me," and he named the master. The magistrate said, "That's enough – call the master. His testimony is worth that of ten thousand people. What he says about you will be enough to give judgment." And the magistrate asked the master, "Do you know this man?"

The master said, "Know him? We are partners, he is my friend. He even visited me one night in the middle of the night. It was so cold that I gave him my blanket. He is using it – you can see. That blanket is famous all over the country; everybody knows it is mine."

The magistrate said, "He is your *friend?* And he steals?"

The master said, "Never! He could never steal. He is such a gentleman that when I gave him the blanket he said to me, 'Thank you, sir.' When he went out of the house, he silently closed the doors. He is a very polite, nice fellow."

The magistrate said, "If you say so, then all the testimonies of the witnesses who have said that he is a thief are canceled. He is freed." The master went out and the thief followed him.

The master said, "What are you doing? Why are you coming with me?"

He said, "Now I can never leave you. You have called me your friend, you have called me your partner. Nobody has ever given me any respect. You are the first person who has said that I am a gentleman, a nice person. I am going to sit at your feet and learn how to be like you. From where have you got this maturity, this power, this strength, this seeing of things in a totally different way?"

The master said, "Do you know that night how bad I felt? You had gone; it was so cold. Without a blanket sleep was not possible. I was just sitting by the window seeing the full moon, and I wrote a poem: 'If I was rich enough I would have given this perfect moon to that poor fellow who had come in the dark to search for something in a poor man's house. I would have given the moon if I had been rich enough, but I am poor myself.' I will show you the poem, come with me.

"I wept that night, that thieves should learn a few things. At least they should inform a day or two days ahead when they come to a man like me, so we can arrange something, so they don't have to go empty-handed. And it is good that you remembered me in the court; otherwise those fellows are dangerous, they may have mistreated you. I offered that very night to come with you and be partners with you, but you refused. Now you want...there is no problem, you can come. Whatever I have I will share with you. But it is not material, it is something invisible."

The thief said, "That I can feel – it is something invisible. But you have saved my life, and now it is yours. Make whatever you want to make of it. I have been simply wasting it. Seeing you, looking in your eyes, one thing is certain – that you can transform me. I fell in love that very night."

Maturity to me is a spiritual phenomenon.

Beyond Psychology, Session 37, April 30, 1987

# THE AUTHOR

# *Osho*

Osho was born in Kuchwada, India, on December 11, 1931. From his earliest childhood, he was a rebellious and independent spirit, challenging all religious, social and political traditions and insisting on experiencing the truth for himself rather than acquiring knowledge and beliefs given by others.

At the age of 21 on March 21, 1953 Osho became enlightened. He says about himself, " *I am no longer seeking, searching for anything. Existence has opened all its doors to me. I cannot even say that I belong to existence, because I am just a part of it.... When a flower blossoms, I blossom with it. When the sun rises, I rise with it. The ego in me, which keeps people separate, is no longer there. My body is part of nature, my being is part of the whole. I am not a separate entity.*"

In the course of his work, Osho has spoken on virtually every aspect of the development of human consciousness. From Sigmund Freud to Lao Tzu, from George Gurdjieff to Gautam Buddha, from the gospels of Jesus to the songs of Kabir, from a multitude of Zen Masters to the fragments of Heraclitus. Osho has distilled from each the essence of what is significant to the spiritual quest of the contemporary human being, based not only on an intellectual understanding but tested against his own existential experience.

He belongs to no tradition, *"I am the beginning of a totally new religious consciousness,"* he says. *"Please don't connect me with the past - it is not even worth remembering."*

His talks to disciples, friends and seekers from all over the world have been published in more than 650 volumes, and translated in over thirty languages. There are over 3,000 of these talks recorded on audio tape, and over 1,700 on video tape. *"My message is not a doctrine, not a philosophy. My message is a certain alchemy, a science of transformation.... Only those few courageous people will be ready to listen, because listening is going to be risky. Listening, you have taken the first step towards being reborn.... The people who remain interested in my work will be simply carrying the torch, but not imposing anything on anybody.... I want them to grow on their own, qualities like love, around which no church can be created; like awareness, which is nobody's monopoly; like celebration, rejoicing, and maintaining fresh childlike eyes. I want people to know themselves, not to be according to someone else - and the way is in."*

On January 19, 1990 Osho left his body. The scope of his work continues to expand as new people discover and become interested in his teachings. Osho last resided in Poona India, where there is currently a flourishing ashram of seekers from all across the globe participating in daily growth, creativity and meditation programs.

# Books by Osho

## *ENGLISH LANGUAGE EDITIONS*

**Early Discourses and Writings**
A Cup of Tea *Letters to Disciples*
From Sex to Superconsciousnes
I Am the Gate
The Long and the Short and the All
The Silent Explosion

**Meditation**
And Now, and Here (Volumes 1&2)
The Book of the Secrets
  (Volumes 1–5) *Vigyana Bhairava Tantra*
Dimensions Beyond the Known
In Search of the Miraculous (Volume 1)
Meditation: the Art of Ecstasy
The Orange Book
  *The Meditation Techniques of*
  *Bhagwan Shree Rajneesh*
The Perfect Way
The Psychology of the Esoteric

**Buddha and Buddhist Masters**
The Book of the Books (Volumes 1–4)
  *The Dhammapada*
The Diamond Sutra  *The Vajrachchedika*
  *Prajnaparamita Sutra*
The Discipline of Transcendence
  (Volumes 1–4)
  *On the Sutra of 42 Chapters*
The Heart Sutra
  *The Prajnaparamita Hridayam Sutra*
The Book of Wisdom (Volumes 1&2)
  *Atisha's Seven Points of Mind Training*

**Indian Mystics:**
**The Bauls**
The Beloved (Volumes 1&2)

**Kabir**
The Divine Melody
Ecstasy – The Forgotten Language
The Fish in the Sea is Not Thirsty
The Guest

The Path of Love
The Revolution

**Krishna**
Krishna: The Man and His Philosophy

**Jesus and Christian Mystics**
Come Follow Me (Volumes 1–4)
  *The Sayings of Jesus*
I Say Unto You (Volumes 1&2)
  *The Sayings of Jesus*
The Mustard Seed
  *The Gospel of Thomas*
Theologia Mystica
  *The Treatise of St. Dionysius*

**Jewish Mystics**
The Art of Dying
The True Sage

**Sufism**
Just Like That
The Perfect Master (Volumes 1&2)
The Secret
Sufis: The People of the Path
  (Volumes 1&2)
Unio Mystica (Volumes 1&2)
  *The Hadiqa of Hakim Sanai*
Until You Die
The Wisdom of the Sands (Volumes 1&2)

**Tantra**
Tantra, Spirituality and Sex *Excerpts*
  *from The Book of the Secrets*
Tantra: The Supreme Understanding
  *Tilopa's Song of Mahamudra*
The Tantra Vision (Volumes 1&2)
  *The Royal Song of Saraha*

**Tao**
The Empty Boat
  *The Stories of Chuang Tzu*

The Secret of Secrets (Volumes 1&2)
*The Secret of the Golden Flower*
Tao: The Golden Gate (Volumes 1&2)
Tao: The Pathless Path (Volumes 1&2)
*The Stories of Lieh Tzu*
Tao: The Three Treasures (Volumes 1–4)
*The Tao Te Ching of Lao Tzu*
When the Shoe Fits
*The Stories of Chuang Tzu*

## The Upanishads
I Am That  *Isa Upanishad*
Philosophia Ultima
*Mandukya Upanishad*
The Supreme Doctrine  *Kenopanishad*
That Art Thou
*Sarvasar Upanishad, Kaivalya
Upanishad, Adhyatma Upanishad*
The Ultimate Alchemy  (Volumes 1&2)
*Atma Pooja Upanishad*
Vedanta: Seven Steps to Samadhi
*Akshya Upanishad*

## Western Mystics
Guida Spirituale  *On the Desiderata*
The Hidden Harmony
*The Fragments of Heraclitus*
The Messiah (Volumes 1&2)
*Commentaries on Kahlil Gibran's
The Prophet*
The New Alchemy: To Turn You On
*Mabel Collins' Light on the Path*
Philosophia Perennis (Volumes 1&2)
*The Golden Verses of Pythagoras*
Zarathustra: A God That Can Dance
*Commentaries on Friedrich Nietzsche's
Thus spoke Zarathustra*
Zarathustra: The Laughing Prophet
*Commentaries on Friedrich Nietzsche's
Thus spoke Zarathustra*

## Yoga
Yoga: The Alpha and the Omega
(Volumes 1–10)
*The Yoga Sutras of Patanjali*
Yoga: The Science of the Soul
(Volumes 1–3) *Original title Yoga: The
Alpha and the Omega (Volumes 1–3)*

## Zen and Zen Masters
Ah, This!
Ancient Music in the Pines

And the Flowers Showered
Bodhidharma The Greatest Zen Master
*Commentaries on the Teachings of the
Messenger of Zen from India to China*
Dang Dang Doko Dang
The First Principle
The Grass Grows By Itself
The Great Zen Master Ta Hui
*Reflections on the Transformation of
an Intellectual to Enlightenment*
Hsin Hsin Ming: The Book of Nothing
*Discourses on the Faith-Mind of Sosan*
Live Zen
Nirvana: The Last Nightmare
No Water, No Moon
Returning to the Source
Roots and Wings
The Search  *The Ten Bulls of Zen*
A Sudden Clash of Thunder
The Sun Rises in the Evening
Take it Easy (Volumes 1&2)
*Poems of Ikkyu*
This. This. A Thousand Times This.
This Very Body the Buddha
*Hakuin's Song of Meditation*
Walking in Zen, Sitting in Zen
The White Lotus
*The Sayings of Bodhidharma*
Zen: The Diamond Thunderbolt
Zen: The Path of Paradox (Volumes 1–3)
Zen: The Quantum Leap
from Mind to No-Mind
Zen: The Solitary Bird,
Cuckoo of the Forest
Zen: The Special Transmission

## Responses to Questions:
*Poona 1974-1981*
Be Still and Know
The Goose is Out!
My Way: The Way of the White Clouds
Walk Without Feet, Fly Without Wings
and Think Without Mind
The Wild Geese and the Water
Zen: Zest, Zip, Zap and Zing

*Rajneeshpuram*
From Darkness to Light
*Answers to the Seekers of the Path*
From the False to the Truth
*Answers to the Seekers of the Path*
The Rajneesh Bible (Volumes 1–4)

**HARDBOUND BOOKS**

# Two Beautiful Books for Contemplation

## A MUST FOR MORNING CONTEMPLATION

5 3/4" x 8 1/4"   406 PAGES
3-89338-104-x

## A MUST FOR CONTEMPLATION BEFORE SLEEP

5 3/4" x 8 1/4"   408 PAGES
3-89338-105-8

The selections in these pages are taken from intimate dialogues between Osho and his disciples and others who came seeking his insight and blessings.  At Osho's suggestion the books are specifically designed to be read upon waking and before entering sleep. The morning contemplations are uplifting and inspiring, encouraging a lively participation in the day to come.  The evening contemplations remind the reader of the beauty and significance of relaxation, expansion, melting, letting go. The books are interspersed with photographs and contain exquisite full color end covers of Osho's art.

"Learn to be more and more silent, learn to be more and more still....
When you are in profound silence you are capable of becoming the host to godliness."

**Available from *Chidvilas, Inc.***

**HARDBOUND BOOKS**

# From the World Tour –
## An Intimate Trilogy of Discourses Given in Uruguay

## BEYOND PSYCHOLOGY

7 1/2" X 8 1/4"   416 PAGE
3-89338-028-

## THE PATH OF THE MYSTIC

7 1/2" X 8 1/4"   462 PAGE
3-89338-040-

## THE TRANSMISSION OF THE LAMP

7 1/2" X 8 1/4"   443 PAGE
3-89338-049-

In this engrossing series of 134 discourses, Osho invites the listener/reader to delve deeply into the essential mysteries of life and discusses a rich variety of methods – including his most profuse exploration of the tool of self hypnosis – that the seeker may experiment with to make the journey to the pulsebeat of meditation that rests within everyone.

*"Silence is the ultimate truth. In silence we meet with existence – words, languages, all create barriers. And to be silent means to be a hollow bamboo. And the miracle is, the moment you are a hollow bamboo, a music descends through you which is not your own. It comes through you; it belongs to the whole. Its beauty is tremendous, its ecstasy – immeasurable. These meetings are just a preparation for that music to descend in you.... And to me, that music is the ultimate experience, the last benediction, the highest flowering of your consciousness."*

**Available from *Chidvilas, Inc.***

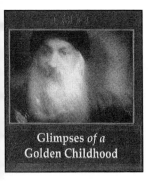

Glimpses *of a*
Golden Childhood

## GLIMPSES
## OF A GOLDEN CHILDHOOD

In what may be the juiciest, most intimate tapestry of talks ever given by an enlightened master, Osho paints the stories of his delightful, inquisitive and mischievous childhood. He began his explorations into truth with an incredible dynamic innocence and courage. With his spirited nature, he questioned every orthodox belief and everyone who blindly espoused or lived by any such beliefs rather than by their own authentic experience. This tapestry contains stories about his encounters with death, his adventures in school and his confrontations with the so called authorities. It is full of hilarious incidences about sex, smoking, religion and dialogues with the local enlightened man in his village. In these sessions, Osho recalls with deep love and respect the connection with his *Nani* (his grandmother, with whom he lived for most of his childhood) who encouraged his every enquiry without prejudice and who was always a source of unconditional love. This book is an invitation to greet each moment of life with the freshness of a child.

7 1/2" X 8 1/2"    553 PAGES + 64 PAGES OF
INTIMATE PHOTOS OF OSHO
3-89338--012-4

## GOLD NUGGETS

This exquisitely designed little book is exactly what its title states: a treasury of gold nuggets – excerpts from talks Osho gave on his world tour.

*"Existence has given me so much. There is no way to pay anything back. There is no word even to express gratitude. The only way is that my every breath should be used in helping people to reach to the same Everest of consciousness."*

4 3/4" X 7 1/2"   185 PAGES
3-89338-107-4

**Available from *Chidvilas, Inc.***

# THE OSHO NEO TAROT

The original artwork of these luminous cards was inspired by Osho's incomparable storytelling. Each of the 60 cards portrays one of life's major lessons as beautifully indicated in a story from Zen, Sufi, Hindu, Tantra, Tibetan, Christian and Greek traditions. Osho breathes life into these ancient teachings, relating them to the challenges of modern living.

An instruction booklet with the complete stories is included. This popular tarot deck makes an excellent gift for fun, inspiration and healing.

3 5/8" X 5 5/8"   60 FULL COLOR CARDS AND BOOKLET
3-8933090-

*"A man becomes a buddha the moment he accepts all that life brings with gratitude."*

**Available from *Chidvilas, Inc.***

**Books, audiotapes, videotapes and photos of Osho are available from the following centers:**

**AMERICA U.S.A**
Chidvilas, Inc
PO Box 17550
Boulder, CO 80308
Ph. 303-449-7811
Fax 303-449-7099
Order Dept. 800-777-7743

**AUSTRALIA**
Osho Meditation
and Mystery School
PO Box 1097
Fremantle. WA 6160
Ph: 61-09-336-2262
Fax 61-09-335-3531

**CANADA**
Publications Osho
1120 Paquette Brossard
Quebec, J4W 2T2
Ph: 514-672-0799

**DENMARK**
Osho Risk Bookstore
Bogballevej 3, 8740
Braedstrup
Ph. 45-75-75-2500

**FINLAND**
Unio Mystica Shop
PO Box 186 Albertinkatu
10 00121 Helsinki
Ph: 358-90-680-1657

**GERMANY**
Osho Verlag GmbH
5-7 Venloer Str.
5000 Cologne 1
Ph. 49-221-574-0743
Fax 49-221-523-930

**INDIA**
Sadhana Foundation
17 Koregaon Park
Poona, 411 001
Ph. 91-212-660-963
Fax 91-212-664-181

**ITALY**
News Services Corporation
Via Teulie 14, 20136
Milano
Ph. 39-02-583-00039

**JAPAN**
Osho Eer
Neo-Sannyas Commune
Mimura Building, 6-21-34
Kikuna, Kohoku-ku,
Yokohama, 222
Ph. 81-45-434-1981
Fax 81-45-434-5565

**NEW ZEALAND**
Rebel Books Mail Order
PO Box 193 Papakura
Ph. 64-09-292-2602

**NETHERLANDS**
Osho Publikaties Nederland
Vianenstraat 48,
1106 DD Amsterdam
Ph. 31-02-6969-372
Fax 31-02-6915-642

**SPAIN**
Distributiones
"El Rebelde" "ES Seralet"
07192 Estellencs
Mallorca-Baleares
Ph. 34-71-410-470
Fax 34-71-719-027

**SWEDEN**
Osho Madhur
Meditation Center
Fridhemsgatan 41 11246,
Stockholm
Ph. 46-08-651-4270
Fax 46-08-651-1709

**UNITED KINGDOM**
Osho Purnima Distribution
OSHO PURNIMA DISTRIBUTION ,
"GREENWISE"
VANGE PARK ROAD
VANGE, BASILDON
ESSEX, SS16 5LA
Tel: 0268 584141

**For a Catalog of Books, Audio
and Video Tapes by Osho
Write or Call:**

*Chidvilas, Inc.*
PO Box 17550
Boulder, CO 80308
303-449-7811

**For Further Information Contact:**

*Osho Commune International*
17 Koregaon Park
Poona, MS 411 001
INDIA